HOW TO MAKE
$1 MILLION DOLLARS
F.A.S.T.:

And Make It Last!

**PLUS 20 great topics from proven
leaders to inspire you to
award winning success!**

*To Jim & Shirley)
From your BROTHER-IN-LAW
Love,
Bob*

BOB KLEIN

How to Make $1 Million Dollars F.A.S.T.:
And Make It Last!

By Bob Klein

PLUS 20 great topics from proven leaders to inspire you to award winning success!

ISBN: to come

Published by Mike Litman's Plug & Play Book Program

Cover Design and Layout by Parry Design Studio, Inc.
www.parrydesign.com

FOREWORD

"How to Make $1 Million Dollars F.A.S.T.: And Make It Last! by Bob Klein is the top Success Tactic in a book full of exciting new ideas. Bob is a rising star in the field of Success. You will love the insights he brings to the Personal Growth and Success field." *Bill Quain, Ph.D.*

"Every new level of success requires a NEW YOU, and Bob Klein helps you get to that next level quickly." *Mike Litman*

When Mike Litman and Bill Quain began the Success Series, they set up a platform to showcase new authors. "There are great thinkers and experts all over the world, and nobody hears their words," says Quain. "Mike and I wanted to change all that. We set out to discover the best new authors, and help them get their messages of hope, victory, courage, and leadership into the hands, heads and hearts of the people who need to read those messages. If you are reading this book, it is no coincidence. But, realize this, without the Success Series, you probably would not be enjoying Bob's writing."

First, Define Success...

Before launching the Success Series, Litman and Quain had to define success! That makes sense, doesn't it? After all, when looking for the best new experts in the filed, it helps to understand what the field covers. The authors define Success in three words: Money, Sunny and Honey. All of the chapters in this book, and in every book in the Success Series are designed specifically to develop success, and to build each reader's desire to achieve it. Each chapter focuses on at least one aspect of Money, Honey or Sunny.

Money

Everyone needs money—and they need a lot of it! But, money isn't just a matter of getting paid for time worked. It needs to be recurring, abundant and created through ingenuity and energy. Money is the cornerstone of success, because it is often the easiest to measure. Both Mike and Bill are fans of money and wealth. In fact, they both derive much of their strategic thinking from Napoleon Hill's classic work, *Think and Grow Rich*.

Mike, Bill and all the authors in the Success Series want YOU to have money. It is one of he leading reasons they created the series.

Sunny

There are three main elements of "Sunny." They are mental, physical and spiritual health. Not many of us can be perfect specimens in each of these three health areas, but we can all maximize our health, and attain a "sunny" outlook on life. Our authors will help you with this pursuit. Let them guide you to a better, more Sunny place in your life.

Honey

"Honey" is our shorthand for Relationships, as in "Honey, I'm home." Strong relationships with friends, family and loved ones are the basis for a successful life. Work on your relationships like you work on your job, or your business, and you will have a happier, healthier and more success-ful life.

The Successful Person Has All Three

There is no question about it, successful human beings have all three elements—Money , Sunny and Honey. They have the financial security they need. They maximize their mental, physical and spiritual health, and they build strong relationships—and work on them daily.

Now, some people may question why "Money" should come first in this list. In fact, many readers and audience members have asked that question. Mike and Bill respond simply, "If there isn't any money, it won't be very Sunny, Honey!" Don't be afraid of any part of success. Each has its place, and you can't live life to its fullest without all three in abundance.

So, join Bob Klein and our other experts on a journey of growth and fulfillment. Build your Money, Sunny and Honey, and build your life's success.

ACKNOWLEDGEMENTS

I would like to acknowledge my wife Lynn Ann Stoner Klein for all her patience and hard work all the time. She is a true help mate I depend on and rely upon on this and all my projects. She is the most generous, unselfish human being I've ever known.

I would also like to acknowledge all those who have helped me with the concepts of the **F.A.S.T. Principle.** These are, but are not limited to, Dan Lewter, former Regional Vice President of Nabisco, Tom Marino, my investment advisor, George Caras, my accountant, Diane Chew, my editor, Mike Litman, Bill Quain, Jack Parry and various other bosses and clients who have helped me along the way.

I would also like to acknowledge our Creator, without whom, the **F.A.S.T. Principle** would have been useless.

Thank you, thank you, thank you.

Sincerest personal regards,

Bob Klein

DEDICATION

This book is dedicated to my wife Lynn Ann Stoner Klein without whom the F.A.S.T. Principle would have been useless. Lynn is my partner and my helpmate. She's the most generous, unselfish human being I've ever known. Just ask our children and grandchildren.

This book is also dedicated to all those people who are interested in increasing their personal wealth, keeping it and leaving a legacy for future generations. I hope our system is inspiring to you. I didn't share our personal story to "brag" about what we've accomplished. I shared it to help illustrate the examples of the F.A.S.T. Principle that have worked so well for us. Plus to motivate you to never, never, never, ever give up, and fight for what's important to you.

If we can help you in any further way, please contact us at the numbers below.

Keep on keeping on, good luck and God Bless!

Bob Klein

Home office number: 215-361-7372
Cell phone number: 215-740-4788
E-mail address: robtklein@aol.com.

TABLE OF CONTENTS

HOW TO MAKE $1 MILLION DOLLARS F.A.S.T.:

And Make It Last!

by Bob Klein

How do you make $1 Million Dollars **F.A.S.T.**? And how do you make it Last? Have you asked those questions of yourself? Do you have good answers? I didn't when I asked myself those questions as my wife and I were starting out as a young married couple. Like so many people, we found we were working so many hours that it was hard to enjoy our life and our growing family. We felt conflicted by the need to bring in a steady income and the need to show our children that life doesn't **HAVE** to be a struggle. But it **WAS** a struggle. And we lived with the fear that we would grow old before we felt financially secure. Then we'd be faced with the challenges of a fixed income at retirement. Sound familiar?

You're not alone. The dream of making $1 Million Dollars flies across the mind of almost every adult at one point in their lives. A small percentage of people achieve that and more by working and slaving and putting it away, but never getting the chance to enjoy it. The April 2011 issue of Money Magazine reports that only 7% of American households ever manage to get to $1 Million Dollars. This is according to research firm Spectrem Group. An even smaller percentage win the lottery or inherit it, though it's often "easy come and easy go." An even smaller percentage might manage to steal it. But what if you could make it legally and painlessly just by working a little smarter rather than a lot harder? Does that sound good to you? Then read on!

I'm going to show you the **F.A.S.T.** method for building wealth if you're willing to do a little planning and take a few calculated risks.

Who Can Benefit from the F.A.S.T. approach?

Would you like to get better control of your life and your finances? Are you just starting out and want to know the best way to plan for your future? Are you nearing retirement and want to preserve your nest egg? No matter what financial or life stage you're in, these tried and true principles can move you towards your dreams.

What is Your Dream?

Why do you want to make $1 Million Dollars? To buy the home of your dreams? To have fancy cars? To attract many friends? To travel around the world? To enjoy retirement? To live debt free? To put your children and/or grandchildren through college? To start your own business, and not have to depend on a corporation? To leave a legacy for your children and grandchildren? To not worry about finances and be able to sleep through the night?

If you said "Yes" to any of the above, the F.A.S.T. approach will help you achieve your goals and dreams.

The F.A.S.T. approach is so simple that many people discount how powerful it can be. But if you're willing to be a little disciplined and a little creative, you too, can end the struggle and enjoy life on the way to building your first Million Dollars.

F   Be Frugal

This may seem obvious, but so many people ignore the power of being reasonable with their expenditures. Try to resist splurging and overspending. Only invest in those things that you need to achieve your objectives. But at the same time, try to look for creative ways to enjoy the pleasures of life.

I didn't have much money when we first started out. I felt like a victim of corporations and employers. One day, I said, "I don't want to live like this any more."

My wife and I have four grown children and four grandchildren. We have always enjoyed many family vacations. But, we didn't always stay in four or five star hotels and eat at the finest restaurants. In the early days, we would travel mostly by car. Once we went to Walt Disney World in Orlando, Florida. All of us packed into our large station wagon (kind of like "National Lampoon's Vacation.") We had a large cooler with sandwiches and soft drinks so we could keep ourselves nourished without having to stop at expensive restaurants to feed us all. When we arrived at our hotels along the way, I would immediately create an in-room "refrigerator" by putting ice in the wastebaskets. By transferring our cooler contents and adding to our supplies from a local food market, we were set for breakfasts and lunches for the duration of our trip. Who needs expensive meals at expensive restaurants? We were happy to be on vacation at a wonderful place. Our grown children still laugh about this way of having our meals on that vacation. Being frugal doesn't mean you can't have fun! But try to resist smoking or drinking alcohol. It debilitates you and your pocketbook.

A Avoid

The second step in the **F.A.S.T.** approach to building your wealth is to avoid taxes as much as possible. Notice I said "avoid," not "evade." One way we found to avoid (or defer) taxes was to invest in real estate. And it started as a hobby. We used to go out after church on Sundays and try to view as many "Open Houses" as we could find. We started buying small rental houses around the largest lake in New Jersey. Then we would advertise them for rent in the classified sections of local newspapers at, or below the going market rental prices.

We focused on giving our tenants a quality experience for a low price. We treated them like royalty. There were always flowers the day they moved in and a nice greeting card welcoming them to their new home. We found contractors who gave us good prices for labor. And we gave our tenants the choice of using the contractors or getting reimbursed after doing the work themselves. My wife even pitched in with repairs when needed. The whole experience was fun for both the tenants and ourselves. And the best thing was, we got to avoid taxes.

All the repairs, upkeep, interest and property taxes were tax deductible, providing a huge savings in the amount of income tax we owed each year. In addition, depreciation was tax deductible. This was a "gift" from the state. We would have been negligent if we had not taken advantage of this legal loophole.

My goal was to pay zero taxes on my federal income tax return, and one year we were able to achieve that.

The best thing about the experience was that it started out as a hobby, something we truly enjoyed. We prided ourselves on having wonderful "landlord – tenant" relationships. And consequently we had some tenants stay in our rental houses for fifteen or twenty years. They were not only tenants, they were friends, too. We were providing a needed commodity, housing, for those who needed it. And we were also building our wealth by avoiding taxes.

Do you have a hobby or interest that you could build into a "side" business that could help you avoid taxes? Do some research on what you could invest in that would provide some valuable deductions. Or think of a service you could provide out of your home that would allow you to deduct part of your mortgage, property taxes, utilities, etc. Take advantage of these "gifts" from the government while having fun and providing for others too.

S Save

The third step in the **F.A.S.T.** approach is to save, save, save. We all know what it means to save money, but not everyone takes advantage of all the ways to do it. To truly build your wealth and build it quickly, you need to save like there's no tomorrow. Save in your 401K accounts, save in your Individual Retirement Accounts (I.R.A.'s), save on all your purchases. Use automatic savings where you can. Save at least 10% of your income.

Look for all the "little ways" to save money that don't require any sacrifice or hardship. Many newer banks will give you a $100 bonus for opening a new savings account with them. We've done this several times. If you have a large purchase to make, you can often open a 12 or 18 month interest-free credit card with the retailer, allowing you to pay in small amounts and invest the rest until the term is up.

And take advantage of the sales and discounts that are offered on everything from food to cars. My wife has a slogan she uses: "Never pay regular retail for anything." And she doesn't. She watches all the ads very closely. She always gets several estimates from contractors before she decides which one to use. She clips coupons for savings at the local supermarkets.

Just remember: "nickel and diming" doesn't mean that you're a cheapskate. In our bedroom we still have a large bowl in which we save all our nickels and pennies. One year, it paid for part of our family vacation. Saving can be fun!

T Tithe

The fourth and final step in the **F.A.S.T.** approach to building wealth is to Tithe. We all need someone or something that is bigger than us in life. This someone could be a cause, a charity, a religion, or something that we could invest in that brings us satisfaction and a return on our investment of time and treasure. We have a friend who supports orphans overseas. She gets such a thrill when she gets notes and photos from the children.

The tithe is that tenth of your income that you give back to God, which enables Him to move on our behalf in the area of blessings. The Bible records numerous accounts of man tithing to God. God is the creator of everything that exists. He owns everything, and we are simply stewards of that which we have been entrusted. The tithe principle is this: "He gives unto us, we give back to Him one-tenth of all that He has blessed us with."

This could be really scary if you have never done it. So the "T" could also stand for "Trust." But once you see the results and the joy it can bring, it'll become second nature. It just takes courage and faith.

It's like the water pump on the old farm back home. You need to put something into it in order to get something back.

I asked my friend Dan Lewter one time, "What do we give: 10% of our gross income or 10% or our income after taxes?" Dan replied, "It depends on how much you want to be blessed." He was right.

"Bring the whole tithe into the storehouse, that there may be food in my house. Test me in this," says the Lord Almighty, "and see if I will not throw open the floodgates of heaven and pour out so much blessing that you will not have room enough for it." Malachi 3:10

"Give, and it shall be given unto you; good measure, pressed down, and shaken together, and running over, shall men give into your bosom. For with the same measure that ye mete withal it shall be measured to you again." Luke 6:38

So, dear readers, there is something out there bigger than you. Figure out what it is, and give a portion of your time, treasure and talents to it. You will be rewarded beyond your wildest imagination.

By the way, your tithes are tax deductible too. More tax savings!

The Future:

The future is very bright for us, and it can be for you too, if you are willing to start using the **F.A.S.T.** approach now. Beginning January 1, 2012 we're required by law to start taking our Required Minimum Distribution from our IRAs. That'll be an average of $6,000 per month. Add that to our two pensions of approximately $4,000 a month, Social Security of $2,000 a month, and you get a pretty decent income of $12,000 a month from multiple streams of income. Our financial advisor gave us a spread sheet showing that we'll never run out of money as long as we make prudent investment decisions and expenditures. (A copy of our required minimum distribution is at the end of the chapter.)

And, No Debt! We own our beautiful two-story home outright. No mortgage. No credit card payments. No car payments.

How do you make it last?

Once you have made your $1 Million Dollars, how do you make it last? There are basically three ways to do this:

1. Continue living by the **F.A.S.T.** principle.

2. Invest wisely. Be more aggressive in your younger, income-producing years.

3. Be more conservative as you approach retirement.

I recently had to tell my investment advisor "Read my lips, No Risk." He got the message when we threatened to take $100,000 that he was managing for us and give it to another advisor. Now, he listens and incorporates our wishes into his investment strategies and tactics for us.

Once you have made your $1 Million Dollars, protect it with all your might. When I was in my 40's, a large Wall Street investment firm lost $500,000 of our money. The vice president kept saying, "Stay the course. It'll come back." I fired them and got another investment advisor. Get one who will listen to you and incorporate your wishes into your investment strategies.

F.A.S.T. Is Better Than "Quick!"

There are so many "Get-rich Quick" schemes on the market today, it's tempting to ignore the basic sound principles in the F.A.S.T. approach to building your wealth. It takes time and discipline to make $1 Million Dollars F.A.S.T. But it's worth it to lead the life you want to lead and leave a legacy for your children and grandchildren.

If you follow these four principles, you'll be able to achieve all your financial goals and objectives, sleep better at night, and have fun along the way!

F – Be Frugal

A – Avoid Taxes

S – Save

T – Tithe

That's all you have to do if you want to make $1 Million Dollars **F.A.S.T.**

Believe me, it works. We have the bank statements proving it.

And just remember, you don't have to do it alone. We didn't. Our "Higher Power" was with us every step of the way.

"For the Lord is a Great God, and a great King above all gods. In His hands are the deep places of the earth: the strength of the hills is His also. The sea is His, and He made it: and His hands formed the dry land." Psalm 95:3-5

R.M.D. Payout Schedule:

		AccountBal	Growth	R.M.D.	Yr.EndBal.
2011	N/A	$975,945.00	$39,037.80	$.00	$1,014,982.80
2012	27.4	$1,014,982.80	$40,599.31	$37,043.17	$1,018,538.94
2013	26.5	$1,018,538.94	$40,741.56	$38,435.43	$1,020,845.07
2014	25.6	$1,020,845.07	$40,833.80	$39,876.76	$1,021,802.11
2015	24.7	$1,021,802.11	$40,872.08	$41,368.51	$1,021,305.68
2016	23.8	$1,021,305.68	$40,852.23	$42,912.00	$1,019,245.91
2017	22.9	$1,019,245.91	$40,769.84	$44,508.56	$1,015,507.19
2018	22	$1,015,507.19	$40,620.29	$46,159.42	$1,009,968.06
2019	21.2	$1,009,968.06	$40,398.72	$47,640.00	$1,002,726.78
2020	20.3	$1,002,726.78	$40,109.07	$49,395.41	$993,440.44
2021	19.5	$993,440.44	$39,737.62	$50,945.66	$982,232.40
2022	18.7	$982,232.40	$39,289.30	$52,525.80	$968,995.90
2023	17.9	$968,995.90	$38,759.84	$54,133.85	$953,621.89
2024	17.1	$953,621.89	$38,144.87	$55,767.36	$935,999.40
2025	16.3	$935,999.40	$37,439.98	$57,423.28	$916,016.10
2026	15.5	$916,016.10	$36,640.64	$59,097.81	$893,558.93
2027	14.8	$893,558.93	$35,742.36	$60,375.60	$868,925.69
2028	14.1	$868,925.69	$34,757.03	$61,625.94	$842,056.78
2029	13.4	$842,056.78	$33,682.27	$62,840.06	$812,898.99
2030	12.7	$812,898.99	$32,515.96	$64,007.79	$781,407.16
2031	12	$781,407.16	$31,256.29	$65,117.26	$747,546.19
2032	11.4	$747,546.19	$29,901.85	$65,574.23	$711,873.81
2033	10.8	$711,873.81	$28,474.95	$65,914.24	$674,434.52
2034	10.2	$674,434.52	$26,977.38	$66,121.03	$635,290.87
2035	9.6	$635,290.87	$25,411.63	$66,176.13	$594,526.37
2036	9.1	$594,526.37	$23,781.05	$65,332.57	$552,974.85
2037	14.1	$552,974.85	$22,118.99	$39,218.07	$535,875.77
2038	13.4	$535,875.77	$21,435.03	$39,990.73	$517,320.07
2039	12.7	$517,320.07	$20,692.80	$40,733.86	$497,279.01
2040	12	$497,279.01	$19,891.16	$41,439.92	$475,730.25
2041	11.4	$475,730.25	$19,029.21	$41,730.72	$453,028.74
2042	10.8	$453,028.74	$18,121.15	$41,947.11	$429,202.78
2043	10.2	$429,202.78	$17,168.11	$42,078.70	$404,292.19
2044	9.6	$404,292.19	$16,171.69	$42,113.77	$378,350.11
2045	9.1	$378,350.11	$15,134.00	$41,576.94	$351,907.17
2046	8.6	$351,907.17	$14,076.29	$40,919.44	$325,064.02
2047	3.1	$325,064.02	$13,002.56	$104,859.36	$233,207.22
2048	2.1	$233,207.22	$9,328.29	$111,051.06	$131,484.45
2049	1.1	$131,484.45	$5,259.38	$119,531.32	$17,212.51
2050	0.1	$17,212.51	$688.50	$17,901.01	$.00

Total R.M.D. Payout: $2,125,409.88

Based on the following assumptions:
1. A 4% annual return
2. No additional distributions are made from the I.R.A.
3. Spouse beneficiary is deemed to treat the I.R.A. as his/her own after the death of the I.R.A. holder
4. There's no guarantee that the rates of return can be achieved

With Him, we cannot fail! Without Him, we cannot succeed!

He's got the whole world in his hands.

For additional information/questions, free advice, seminars, contact us using the contact information below:

Bob was born and raised in the Deep South, Mississippi and Alabama. His first jobs were picking cotton and working on Mississippi River tug boats. Later in college, he was a radio announcer.

He served three years in the United States Marine Corps, stationed in San Diego and Iwakuni, Japan. He worked for the Far East Network and was the sports editor for the base magazine, the Tori Teller.

He's been married to his wife for 28 years, and has four adult children and four grandchildren, the light of his life.

Bob spent thirty four years with Nabisco. His most recent assignment was Director of National Training. Then he spent three years as Vice President of Porter Henry & Company in New York City and five years with Wyeth Pharmaceuticals Company as Director of Global Training.

At Wyeth, he trained more than 5,000 professionals in 40 different countries. His programs have been translated into more than a dozen different languages.

He earned his Bachelor's Degree with Distinction from San Diego State University and his Master's Degree from California State University. He did doctoral work at the Fielding Institute in Santa Barbara, California.

He's an active member of his Episcopal Church, and has served on the vestry and as Junior Warden and Senior Warden and head lay reader. He also conducts worship services at various retirement communities and nursing homes.

To reach Bob to schedule a speech or consultation, contact him directly at:

Bob Klein
201 Federal Court
Harleysville, PA 19438

Home Office: 215-361-7372
Cell Phone: 215-740-4788
FAX Number: 215-361-3111

E-mail: robtklein@aol.com

You Don't Need To Get It Right, You Just Need To Get It Going

by Mike Litman

People often ask me, "Mike, what is the big secret to your success?" The answer is easy, and anyone who has read one of my books, or heard me speak, or worked directly with me in a coaching program, knows the answer. The one thing that I always focus on. The one thing that I'm obsessed with:

You don't have to get it right, you just have to get it going.

I don't just *say* this to my clients and my customers. I believe it and live it every day of my life. I focus on this one thing because that's what has made ME successful and I want to help you *get* it going and *keep* it going in the right direction.

I've found 7 keys to moving ahead with your dreams and your goals.

These 7 keys catapulted me from an unknown radio talk show host to a best-selling author, consultant and coach.

Now, I offer these keys to you. Use them to reach your dreams. You don't have to get it right – you just have to get it going and keep it going!

1. Trying to Get An "A" Keeps Our Dreams Held Hostage

A lot of us are held captive by our past experiences. In school, we were all taught that we had to do our best. And many of us were taught that we had to get "A's."

Do you still have that feeling? Are you still held captive by what others think about your work, or your dreams, or your desires? Are you doing a lot of extra work, trying to get an "A" before you put yourself out there into the world?

I see it all the time. Instead of writing a good book and getting it out on the market, an author will rewrite the same book and never sell a copy. Or a speaker will practice a presentation again and again, and instead of delivering it to a paying audience, he decides to add "just one more slide."

In your search for the "A" you end up with an "F" in success.

The following story taught me how taking action vs. waiting to get it right put me directly on the path to success.

When I was 26 years old, I started a radio show called *"Conversations With Millionaires."* Nobody knew who I was. I only had three listeners on my show – my mother, my father and me! Yet every week I found a millionaire to interview, and I recorded the entire show. I did it week after week.

Was I ready to be a radio host? Would I have gotten an "A" if I was being graded? Absolutely not But, what would have happened if I had waited until I was good enough to get an "A?" I would never have gotten it going.

Did the radio show make me wealthy? Yes. You see, I took all those recorded interviews with millionaires and put them into a book, and the book, *Conversations With Millionaires*, became a #1 Best-Seller.

But once again – would a teacher have given me an "A" for that book? No! When I first published *Conversations With Millionaires* it had typos. TYPOS! But I decided it was more important to get it out there so I was able to achieve an "A++" in the things I really wanted—my dreams.

If you think you have to get an "A"—that you have to get it perfect before you can go for your dreams, just look around you. NO ONE is doing it perfectly. Go into any business in your neighborhood and watch them. They aren't perfect, yet customers give them money – lots of money.

Trying to get an "A" keeps your dreams held hostage. Get it going and release your dreams to the world.

2. Every Level Of Success Demands A Different YOU

Are you ready to hear this? This one actually has two messages in it, and both of them are critically important to your success. The first is obvious: if you want to move up a level, you need to think, act and believe different things than you do at your present level of success. You need to be a new YOU. If you want things to be different, then YOU must be different.

Success is a journey, and we need to enjoy that journey. We also need to change and grow so that we can KEEP our success going.

Have you ever seen one of those television shows about lottery winners who go broke? It happens all the time. You see, they didn't suffer from a lack of money, they suffered from a lack of growth. They didn't change their actions and thinking when they won the money, and so they lost it.

The second part of this secret is not so obvious. But, it is equally important. Look at the heading. It says "Every LEVEL of Success..." Do you see the significance in this wording?

Most people see success as a giant leap from where they are now, to some place else they want to be. But, success isn't made up of giant leaps. It is made up of steps. And levels. You need to move from one level to the other.

But so many people stop moving forward because they think they're not moving fast enough. They're trying to get it right – and they STOP keeping it going.

Be willing to grow and change with each level of success. Be willing to take small, consistent steps forward and you WILL keep it going.

You don't have to get it "right"—you don't have to move forward in leaps and bounds. You just have to get it going, and keep it going.

3. End Procrastination Forever – Build A Vision

Do you know why you procrastinate? Do you know why you put off doing things? It's because the pain of doing them is greater than the pain of not having what you want. But if your dream, or your vision for your life is strong, then the pain of NOT HAVING it will be stronger than the pain of doing those things.

You need a dream. It should be clearly defined, and it should be yours. I can't tell you what your dream should be. You have to define it for yourself.

But some people never get going because they can't decide on their dream. They're trying to make sure they're following the "right" dream. But—remember the one thing that I always focus on. It applies here, too. You don't have to get it right, you just have to get it going.

Maybe you don't have every aspect of your dream mapped out. But I bet you know ONE THING you could do that would put you on a new "track." That would keep you from bouncing from one side of the train to the other and send you off in a new direction.

And as you get started, your dream will get bigger and clearer and you'll start to want it so badly that you'll be willing to do almost anything to get it. And your procrastination will end. Forever.

Start to build a vision by doing just one thing. I don't know what your ONE THING is, but I'll bet you do! It is that certain something that you absolutely KNOW would increase your business and your success. You don't do it, and you keep putting it off. Sometimes, you just ignore it. But, it doesn't go away.

Do that ONE THING, and do it right now. Do it well, but don't worry about doing it perfectly. Don't worry about getting the ONE THING right, just get it going.

4. Get Passionate About the Problems You Can Solve

The only way to achieve your dreams is to solve problems. You must solve other people's problems in order to solve yours. Why is that? Because when you solve people's problems, they give you rewards, and those rewards solve YOUR problems.

But, you have to carefully determine which problems you can solve. What do you do, or what CAN you do that other people need? What problems are out there that need your special brand of solving?

Look for the PAIN and you will find the problems. Then, choose the problems you can solve and focus ONLY on them. Don't get distracted.

I work with a lot of coaches. The most successful coaches I know have found a solution to some BIG problem, and then devoted themselves to helping others solve that problem. Remember, you aren't in this to solve YOUR problems, you want to solve problems for paying customers and clients.

For example, one of my clients wrote a book about "reducing stress." Is STRESS a problem for many, many people? It is, of course, but most people don't think, "My problem is that I have stress." Instead, they are thinking, "My problem is that I'm always tired, and my kids and husband just don't understand that."

Do you see the difference? If my client went around trying to solve the stress problem, no one would buy her book. If she solves the why doesn't anyone understand just how hard I work problem, she can do very well.

Just beware of the trap that, once again, stops too many people from getting going and helping others. They think they have to be the expert in order to solve other's problems. But you only have to know 1% more than they do in order to help them. Just 1%.

So remember: your readers don't have "stress" pains, they have "I need help and understanding" pains. And you can help them by knowing only 1% more, and getting it going.

5. You Were Not Put Here To Serve EVERYONE, Just Someone

One of the great things about concentrating on the things you do best is that you don't have to do it for everyone. You only need to do it for the people who will appreciate it and who will reward you for it.

Some people should not be your customers or clients. You can't solve their problems. Some people don't LIKE the way you work, even if you CAN solve their problems.

You aren't looking to help everyone, you are just looking for the people who will celebrate you. These are the people who will make you successful.

Did you ever hear of the 80/20 rule? It says that 80% of your rewards come from just 20% of your customers or clients. If this is true, and I believe it is, then why do you try so hard to hang on to the 80% of the people who are not giving you rewards?

I see this happen all the time, and not just to new business people. Some people are afraid to lose any clients or customers. So, they waste a lot of time and money, trying to keep customers who were never going to make them successful anyway. They keep trying to get it right for everybody – and they stop themselves from keeping it going.

Keep growing your business overall so that you always get new clients. If you do this, you will keep growing that 20% who will make you successful.

You don't have to get it right for everybody – get it right for someone and keep it going!

6. Develop L-O-V-E-R-A-G-E – –

What is L-O-V-E-R-A-G-E? It is the boost you get when you give to others. The word is a cross between love and leverage and these are two things you simply MUST have in your business life if you are going to reach your dreams.

You need to love others, and solve their problems. Do you know how many people need your help right now? There are thousands and thousands. They are in pain.

And when you use your special talents to help them, if you love them, you will ease their burdens and make them feel better.

They, in turn will love you back. Now, that probably sounds strange to you doesn't it? After all, I am a business person, right? I am not supposed to be looking for love from customers and clients.

But, I am!

When I solve one person's problems, they will tell others about me – for two reasons. First, they want their friends, families and acquaintances to do better, and second, they want ME to do better. This is leverage, and when it is done with love, it is L-O-V-E-R-A-G-E.

And L-o-v-e-r-a-g-e can keep you going when you hit the biggest obstacle to your success: yourself!

Put this picture into your mind. You are walking around with a load of suitcases. They are full of negative thoughts, bad ideas, other people's feelings about you, and your fears. On top of all those bags is a small one that is very, very heavy. It is the one that has the thought: "I need to get this perfect or people will laugh at me."

Now, picture yourself running for a train. That train is going to take you to the best place in the whole world. You will have money, time, friendships, strong relationships and great health. But, the train is starting to pull out of the station, and you are still a half block away.

So you have a choice. Hold on to the baggage, or drop it all, especially that small heavy bag of "perfection" and run for that train. You can hold on to that bag or remember the people who are in pain. The people who need your help. It's your choice

L-o-v-e-r-a-g-e can help you to get it going and keep it going!

7. Never, EVER Go To Bed The Same Person You Were When You Woke Up

Let me leave you with this one thought. Every day is yours to use, or lose. I already told you that you don't have to get it right, you just have to get it going, and keep it going.

I told you to stop trying to get "A's." I told you that success has levels and you must be willing to grow and change, but also take your success one step at a time. I told you to solve problems, celebrate some people (and they will celebrate you back) and I told you to use L-O-V-E-R-A-G-E.

If you do those things, you WON'T be the same person at the end of the day. You will meet new winners and learn from them. You will give and receive love and rewards. You will grow by easing others' pains.

THAT is my gift to you. Put everything else into that baggage, drop it and run for the train.

So, do you want to wait until it is just right? Or, would you rather get it going - right now - and keep it going?

I probably didn't even have to ask you that, did I?

Mike Litman is the #1 best-selling author of 'Conversations with Millionaires'. Over the last 10 years Mike has helped over 250,000 people unleash their greatness. Mike has also shared the stage with many well-known success experts such as Jim Rohn, Mark Victor Hansen, T. Harv Eker, Loral Langemeier, Stephen Pierce, and many others. He's also been featured on TV and many business magazines.

Over the last 5 years, Mike has also shared his proven system to turning your passion into Internet profit with thousands of individuals. If you're committed to getting going and changing your life, grab Mike Litman's free success newsletter at http://www.mikelitman.com

THE BIG SELLING SECRET

If you want to sell, know how they buy.

by Bill Quain

The internet, computers, blogs, ebooks and self-publishing have created a huge problem for authors, coaches and speakers. It is now almost too easy to create content. However, it hasn't gotten any easier to *sell* that content to the people who need it. Unfortunately, this has created a huge backlog of exceptional material. Because of this, very few people are making money on their hard work—and potential readers and clients are starving for good, useable information.

Are you a coach with excellent material, but with no visible income to show for it? Have you written ebooks and blogs, but are unable to sell them? Perhaps you are an expert who can help people with their problems, but you're unable to reach them, or even worse, unable to get them to *pay* you for your help and knowledge. If any of these situations apply to you, you are not alone.

Like thousands of other "Content Kings and Queens," you spent a lifetime overcoming adversity and building up a huge store of advice and instruction. But, while many people tell you just how good and helpful your material is, you have not found a way to turn your knowledge into cash.

What a shame! You did all that work, and now you have nothing to show for it. You are brimming with great information, yet no one seems to think that your information is worth much. How could that be possible, and what can you do to change it? In this chapter, I am going to help you overcome the biggest obstacle in modern coaching/author/expert marketing: turning your hard-earned, hard-learned knowledge into a fantastic income stream. Are you ready to make the leap from *content creation* to *cash creation*?

What Happened to the Internet?

If you are like most experts and coaches, you are on many email lists from "Marketing Gurus" who will gladly sell you the latest "Top Ten Tips" for doing_____" (Just fill in the blank. Someone is selling it to you.) You could easily go broke by buying all the great strategies that others have used to make money.

Do some of them work? Well, I am sure that some of them do. In fact, I am certain that *all of them work some of the time.* There are some great minds out there. When they say, "This technique really made a difference. The first time I used it, I sold ____ copies of my product. The second time I used it, I DOUBLED my old record. The third time I used it, Google (or Yahoo, or whatever) threatened to shut me down because the volume was too high."

Are they telling the truth? I know a lot of these people and, yes, I believe they are. You see, their techniques are part of a larger plan they have. They apply time-tested marketing and selling techniques that really do work – *in the right circumstances, and for the right products or services.*

These gurus are using the internet to market and sell their products. So, why can't you use it successfully? Wasn't the internet supposed to make it easy to find your audience, sell them hundreds and thousands of products, and make a fortune? What happened to the internet? Why isn't it working for the average author/expert/speaker?

Hey, the internet is free, right? It doesn't cost anything to use it, so you should be able to start making money right away. EVERYONE is using the internet. Your buyers are looking online sixteen hours per day, right? They have money bulging out of their pockets, and they are looking for YOUR stuff right now, aren't they? Isn't it just a matter of creating a nice website, doing a few SEO tricks and then waiting for the checks (or at least, the PayPal notices) to come rolling in?

The problem isn't the internet, the problem is that most people don't know the barriers that are standing between them and their money.

Barriers... What Barriers?

If you have a product or service, and it is not selling, then there are barriers. Actually, if you ARE selling your products, there are still barriers – you just found some way to overcome these barriers. Many would-be salespeople stop selling the minute they encounter an obstacle. For example, if your customers think your price is too high, do you simply give up? If you do, you wouldn't be the first one to do it. (Instead of giving up, find a way to increase the value of your offer until it overcomes the barrier.)

However, too many experts and authors look at the internet as a "barrier-free" sales space. They use the free web space to overload the customers with facts and figures, all designed to convince a generally skeptical and unwilling audience to buy a book or program.

But guess what? Your customers are not going to wade through a lot of facts. They don't have the time to sort through all your great information. Customers today, especially those that use the internet, want fast relief for their problems, not information. They want to be WOWED, not sold. They want extraordinary value and excitement. Most of all, they want a feeling of **relief.** They want to know that someone "Gets It" and understands exactly what they need. And, they want all that right now.

If they don't get that feeling, they will throw up barriers that will prevent you from ever reaching YOUR goals for wealth, fame and freedom.

What About The Big Selling Secret?

In the title of this book, I promised you that I would reveal "The Big Selling Secret." I will do that, but first, I want to make sure you are ready for it. If I just give it to you, it won't do you much good. You need to have some preparation.

So, before revealing The Big Selling Secret, let me tell you what it will do for you, and why it is so important.

When you understand The Big Selling Secret, you will have the key that unlocks any barrier to sales. How does that sound? If you know The Big Selling Secret, you will not have to worry about learning the next big selling technique. You won't get sidetracked when someone says, "This is the tip that will make you rich." You will know right away if it will work for you, with this product, at this time.

Okay, now you are ready, and here is The Big Selling Secret:

"If you want to sell something, you need to know who is buying it."

Now, I know what you are thinking to yourself: "That's it? That is the Big Selling Secret? Is this guy crazy? Who doesn't know that?"

I admit, The Big Selling Secret does sound too simple. It sounds like everyone should know it, doesn't it? And, on the surface, it may not seem like it is much help to you. But, I can tell you this. I used the Big Selling Secret to sell over TWO MILLION books, and to travel worldwide giving paid presentations to thousands and thousands of people.

Because I use The Big Selling Secret, I have been "sighted" in airports and hotels. (People recognized me from my picture on the back of my books.) One man even did a double take on a cruise ship in the Caribbean Sea when he heard me talking to my daughter outside a restaurant on the main deck. He knew my voice – but not my face – from some audios I had recorded.

Because I know The Big Selling Secret, I was able to buy a huge house right off the beach in a shore resort, had a great fishing boat that enabled my daughters to win a tournament in Miami that qualified my older daughter to fish in the World's Championships – twice. In fact, knowing The Big Selling Secret enabled my wife to take 19 years off work while we raised our children.

Finally, because I knew The Big Selling Secret, I was ready when Mike Litman asked me to work with him to establish his "Plug & Play Book Program." Folks, when one of the top marketers and coaches in the WORLD notices you, it means you have something good going on. Mike Litman knows the value of The Big Selling Secret, and he has used it to make millions of dollars, and to change his family's lives forever.

So, simple as it may be, The Big Selling Secret can change YOUR life as well.

Bill, I don't Get It Yet...

I understand. You don't quite understand what The Big Selling Secret is, and how it will work for you. Let me explain it a little more with some examples.

Let me tell you about an episode from my favorite comic strip – Dilbert. *Dilbert* is talking to his Dog, Dogbert. Dogbert says, "I am going to write a book about Compulsive Shoppers." What do you know about Compulsive Shoppers?" says Dilbert. Dogbert's answer sums up The Big Selling Secret. "I know that Compulsive Shoppers buy books!"

You see, Dogbert had it figured out. He was going to write books for people who BUY books. Isn't that simple? But, doesn't it make so much sense? Are you writing books (or whatever you produce) for people who buy books, or are you writing books (or whatever you produce) because it is something that **you** want to do, or because **you** think people "need it?" If you are doing it for any other reason than "people buy this stuff," then you are about to make a big mistake.

My Hero in the Book Writing Biz

Let me tell you about Bob Harris, one of my heroes in the book writing biz. Bob owned an Association Management company in Florida. An

Association Management company provides services for Associations that might not be large enough to have their own staffs, but who need a lot of services to keep on operating. Bob also co-authored a book with me in the early days of my writing career—before I discovered The Big Selling Secret.

One Monday, Bob called me to tell me he had written ten books over the weekend. No, I didn't just make a mistake. I wrote "ten" because that is what Bob told me he did.

I was stunned. This was way before the internet, so I had no idea how he could do it. He wrote books that would help the members of the associations he ran. For example one of them was about disposing of waste oil at gas stations. (He ran the Gas Station Owners of Florida Association – or some name like that.) Bob then sent out a mailer (remember, this is pre-internet) to all the members of all the associations. He told them about the ten book titles, and how to order them.

Now, let me let you in on Bob's secret. He didn't actually write ten books. He wrote ten book titles. As people ordered the books, he wrote the ones they ordered. If no one ordered a title, he didn't write the book! If only a few people ordered the title, he wrote back and said, "Sorry, this title is out of print." Bob didn't make a killing with this strategy, but he did pretty well. But, do you know what Bob did not do? He did not waste any of his time! He only wrote the books that people were buying.

That is WHAT They Are Buying, But What About WHO Is Buying?

Today, anyone can find out *what* people are buying. Just look on the internet or on Amazon. But how do you find out *who* is buying your type of product? That is the key.

To discover who is buying, look for the problem that the product solves. Then, simply figure out who has that problem. Those are the people buying your product or service.

For example, suppose you have some expertise in paying fewer taxes. You look on the internet and see a number of books on the subject. Apparently, there is some demand for this product. Some of the authors have high Amazon rankings, indicating that they are selling books. But, who is buying them?

Well, everyone who works has a tax problem. (The problem is that most of us do not want to pay taxes!) But some people are not interested in reading a book for a solution. Low-income earners are probably not going to spend money to learn about reducing taxes. Conversely, *high* income earners may also not be interested because they have tax specialists who do it for them. That leaves middle income families, and you might narrow it down to high-middle earners.

However, in the U.S. it is difficult for wage earners to save money on taxes. It is easier for entrepreneurs and the self-employed to do it. So, you narrow your search even more and discover that this is the most significant group. You decide to write a book for this specific sub segment, because they are the ones who buy books on the subject.

Do you see what we did as we searched for the problem that might cause people to look for this subject? We began to define the market we were interested in – not because of *our* interests, but because of *their* problems. The Big Selling Secret is all about the *buyer* not the seller.

The Other Side of the Secret

Now, I am going to share something with you that will help you become wealthy. It is something that Mike Litman shared with me. In fact, when he showed me how to do this, it completely changed the way I looked at The Big Selling Secret.

Remember, The Big Selling Secret is *"if you want to sell something, you need to, know who is buying."* Now, take that one step farther and you can make some real money. This is The Big Selling Secret's BIG SECRET.

"When you find out who is buying, build the funnel."

What is "The Funnel?" It is the system that takes your clients from a one-product purchase to a multiple-product, fast-growth success story. In other words, don't think of selling them a product as the end of the relationship. Do your customers have just one problem? No! Use your first sale as a foot-in-the-door. When you sell them a product (a book, program, presentation, whatever) you have established credibility with your clients. Now, ask them if they would like to do more.

This is why we call this "The Funnel." A lot of people fall into the wide mouth of the funnel. You're looking for the people who want to solve more problems. They go deeper into the funnel. It is narrower, and more specific. Instead of giving them general problem-solving help, you are focusing your efforts, and building their success more rapidly and completely. You are also making more money. Everyone is happy.

Remember Those Barriers

A few pages ago, I was talking about barriers to sales. Folks, let me tell you what Mike Litman told me: "The biggest barriers do not come from the customers, they come from you." YOU are afraid to ask for more money. YOU are afraid to "bother" people. YOU are afraid of losing customers.

Don't worry about it. LOSE some customers. If you are not losing customers it is because you are running a charity.

Find the clients who want to celebrate you, and celebrate them. WOW them with value, but make it so valuable that they will reward you with wealth as they grow and prosper.

Does it work? I can answer that question for you with ease. "Yes."

What did it take for me to grow, change and build my business? I had to break down the barriers. Of course, the barriers were easy to find, because they were all in one place—my own mind.

Remember The Big Selling Secret. Find the people who buy, because they have your money.

Bill Quain has written 19 books, and sold more than 2 million copies, in 20 languages. He is the Director of Mike Litman's Plug & Play Book Program, and helps others achieve their biggest dreams—becoming a recognized expert by writing a book. Bill is the co-author of Write Fast, Publish Cheap, & Sell More!. To speak with Bill, and to learn more about the Plug & Play Book Program, send him an email at bill@mikelitman.com or phone him at (609) 300-2110.

Bill was a college professor for more than twenty-five years, and he applies his teaching skills to the Plug & Play program, to help anyone finish their book. He knows just how difficult it can be to get started on a book project. Together with Mike Litman, Bill can take a newbie writer from concept to published book in just 30 days.

If you have a book inside you, Bill will get it from your head to the paper, and from paper to published. Call him at (609) 399-2119 today.

7 AWESOME STEPS TO REACH YOUR GOALS

by Patti Armus, RN

The idea of S.M.A.R.T. goals has been around for a long time: Specific, Measurable, Achievable, Realistic and Timely. I have used this strategy myself and have recommended it to my clients in the past. However, I have found it insufficient in helping to specify what the goals should be and how to attain them. By using the AWESOME model, it not only enables you to establish your goals with more clarity and conviction, but it actually provides a roadmap to get you through each of the steps necessary to reach those goals.

A **Actualize and define your need or desire!** By visualizing what you want your end result to be and seeing yourself living that result, it becomes more real. When your brain can truly see something in 3 dimensions, it views it as being attainable. When you take the time to make your dreams reality in your mind's eye – seeing it, touching it, tasting it, savoring it – your success in achieving that goal becomes more do-able.

Sit back and close your eyes. Think of something you want. Something small. Maybe it's an Oreo™ cookie. Visualize that cookie right now. See the chocolate sandwich with the raised letters. See the word, Oreo™. See the ridges encircling the edges. Now feel it. Feel the raised edges. Turn it around in your hand, notice the white cream center. Smell the chocolate smell. Picture twisting the two sandwich halves and separating the cookie. Now imagine sharing that cookie with someone.

I wonder how many of you will have an Oreo™ within the next week…

W **Write it down!** I tell this to my clients all the time. Write down your goals. What do you want to accomplish? What is your heart's desire? Write it down. Write it in a journal or a diary, write it on a sticky note and put it on the bathroom mirror, write it on a white board, write it in magnets on the fridge. Whatever you do, keep it where you can see it all the time. Writing it down does several things for you. First, it helps you to clarify what it is you want. The words make the thought more clear. It's the difference between looking at something through an opaque screen and looking at it up close and personal. Seeing the words in front of you brings it back to the previous step, which is actualizing it. When you read the statement, "I want an Oreo™ cookie," you know you really want it. You can't trick yourself or talk yourself out of it quite as easily as if it were just a thought. (Not good if you're trying to diet; use different imagery.)

E **Energize it!** Get excited about what you want. Don't just make it a statement. Treat it like an event. Tell as many people as you can what you want. Enlist their support, help, and encouragement to help you on your way. Then, get going. Your dreams, desires and goals mean nothing if you don't act on them. Continual movement toward your goals is essential to reaching them. Take action now. It doesn't have to be a big action; it just has to be something. Small steps are easy to make and require little effort. Take action now.

S **See your success!** Celebrate getting what you want. See the balloons and streamers, hear the noisemakers. Feel the energy of the crowd as you bask in their admiration of your ability to realize your dreams. Picture the end result. Where are you once your goals have been reached? Make your goals more real and attainable by visualizing yourself living them. Where are you? How do you look once your goal is reached? How do you feel? What new direction can your life take once your current goals are met? How can that lead to new goals?

O **Open your mind!** Accept all options as possible. Don't second- guess yourself, don't sell yourself short. To move forward with your goals, you need to leave negative thoughts behind. Establish a daily routine of positive self-talk and choose to work through fear and adversity. The key to success is belief in yourself. Find someone to help get you past the times you feel like giving up, whether they push you, as a friend or family member might, or pull you, as a mentor might. Never believe you need to do it alone. In fact, the belief that you have to do it "on your own" is the true nemesis of goal attainment. Look at all the most successful people you can think of. Not one of them "did it" without the help, guidance, or words of encouragement from others. Follow their lead, and your road will be much easier to follow. Surround yourself with people who can appreciate your vision and can help you reach your goals. Don't give in to the nay-sayers.

M   **Measure your success!** Don't think you have to wait until you've reached your goals to consider yourself successful. Each and every step along the way that moves you closer to the end result is a success and a reason to celebrate. If there are ten, five, or even one thing you must do to reach your goal, each thing accomplished is a success. Make sure to put rewards in your plan to reach your goals. Make your rewards frequent and desirable. Get others involved in your celebrations, as well. It's hard to really celebrate by yourself. Celebration is all about the interaction with others to establish a sense of well-being and joy.

E   **Every day!** You need to review your goals each and every day so you never lose sight of them. Don't get caught up in day to day activities and forget your goals. Review them each day and take one small step toward reaching them. Step by step, one day at a time. By practicing to reach your goals every day, you develop new habits that bring you closer to those goals. Write your progress every day, as well. Acknowledge your small, daily successes. Celebrate every little step you take. If you skip a day because "life happens," get back on track the next day you can.

Make your mantra **AWESOME** and you'll see more dreams realized. Goal-setting is important, but by choosing to be **AWESOME**, you will find it easier to determine which goals to work towards and make it easier to take the steps necessary to reach them.

Each of these **AWESOME** guidelines will aid you in taking the steps necessary to set, move towards and reach your goals. Reading this every day is like having your own cheering section. You have the ability to live your dreams. Take small steps, and make small, easy to follow changes. Do something positive every day and your dreams will become your reality.

Reread this every day to help remind you of the power you have to do what you want and be who you want to be. Be as detailed as you can in your description of what you want to attain. Write it down using words that evoke all of your senses. See it. Feel it. Hear it. Smell it. Touch it. Be it.

You have The Power to change. You have The Power to choose. Choose TO BE The Power.

Patti Armus is a registered nurse and health coach with a specialty in cardiac health. In addition to individual coaching she works with small to mid-sized business to develop workplace wellness programs. She has also designed and implemented education and precepting programs, public access defibrillator, and cardiac rehab programs. She is a certified American Heart Association BLS, AED, and First Aid instructor and does training and certification by appointment. Patti is the President/CEO of My CardioResource and My-Med-Keeper.
www.mycardioresource.com/sq
www.my-med-keeper.com

LIZARDS, WIZARDS, HORSES AND HUMANS

From Corporate Burnout to a Life Inspired

by Barbara Alexander

I t all started at Barnes and Noble. I had a cup of coffee and ended up with a book that unbeknownst to me, would change the direction of my life forever. It was titled: The Tao of Equus, A Woman's Journey to Healing and Transformation Through the Way of the Horse. Of course, there are no coincidences.

Joseph Campbell said, "It is by going down into the abyss that we recover the treasures of life. Where you stumble, there lies your treasure."

My 'treasure' seemed to be found in achieving corporate goals, fulfilling clients' needs and caring for my family. Keeping up with the things that inspired me was an exciting adventure, reaching for the incredible feeling of doing more, doing better than I had done before and continuously moving forward, but something insidious had slowly been changing.

Over time, I had begun to lose my energy, and my inspiration had long left the stage! I ignored the warning signs that my body had given me until one day I realized, that I just wasn't happy anymore. So what had shifted and why didn't I notice, long before this, that I was losing the joy in my life?

Inner Lizards – Bouts of Doubt

Most of us put up with many things before we are willing to make a change. It's the ever-increasing discomfort that makes us reach for the new doors to life-breathing inspiration. So how much discomfort is enough before we are ready?

The Inner Lizard, referring to one of the most primitive layers of our brain, sends out warnings to keep us out of danger and is thought to link to the neural structure that evolved in early vertebrates. Listening to the Inner Lizard leaves us believing that we don't have an option that there is not enough to go around, that we can't get what we need, and that we may lose something we want.

These fragments of conditioned patterns cause us to fixate on what is wrong. We've all experienced bouts of doubt in what is commonly called the self-saboteur. We tend to turn on mental tape loops from the past, laced with 'things we should have done,' 'could have done,' and 'aren't doing well enough.'

The problem is that the Inner Lizard blocks us from feeling our way to a better life experience. It inhibits the path to the life we dream about and we can end up with a feeling of being stuck where we are.

Inner Wizards

Having found your inner guide, you have found yourself.

I had overridden my 'Inner Wizard' and had put personal self-care and self-awareness on the back burner for when I had more time, but no matter how I may have muffled the sound, it was always there boundless, ever present, waiting for me to listen.

Through extensive research, we are learning that there is infinite wisdom in every cell of the human body; however, most of us have no idea how to access this 'Inner Wizard' in our everyday lives. We are just beginning to learn how to tune into in to this silent, personal awareness that provides the best answers for our health, well-being and the ultimate satisfaction of our Soul. Getting to the place where we can hear who-we-really-are—unencumbered and clear—seems to be a common challenge.

I knew I needed to change but I was not sure what was wrong or how to fix it. Who was qualified to help me on this most intimate of journeys to become that me I wanted to be? That was when I found the book that serendipitously led me to my first personal retreat, but I had no idea of what I was about to experience.

Horses and Humans

My first encounter was with a magnificent horse that was skilled in the art of allowing his own authentic nature to be fully focused and in the moment, all 1,200 pounds of him! I was mesmerized by his presence.

It was as if everything else had fallen away, just him and just me. It was exhilarating, and I felt so alive!

Many of the people attending this retreat had never experienced horses this closely. We had no idea of what to expect, but the outcome started an extraordinary shift that has helped to reclaim the person I was meant to be.

A rush of clarity and serenity unleashed inside of me, along with the onset of my own self-awareness. I was seeing myself mirrored through the eye of the horse. While it took a few moments to stop resisting the possibility of what was actually happening, I realized that this was the equine-influenced shift in consciousness that I had just been reading about.

Horses do not project their opinions of us as good or bad, they simply mirror, with discerning awareness, each person's individuality. They sense our heart rate and blood pressure as opposed to what we may portray, for instance acting like we are in control or that we have no fear.

Unlike dogs, cats and other predators, horses are highly intuitive and responsive because of their instinctual "prey" awareness. They sense our nonverbal energy, the messages that we are continuously, and involuntarily emitting. Because of this ability, horses shift their behavior the split second we energetically shift ours, thereby teaching us precisely what we need to learn in the moment, that is, **if** we are ready to learn.

The Vibration Between Two Beings

This unforeseen equine teacher, like many spiritual teachers, appeared in my life in perfect time. He patiently taught me how to shift my physical energy forward and back as we played with the experience of mutual respect and all of its subtleties. His patience and persistence were amazing, and if I had not experienced it for myself, it would have been hard to believe.

As the retreat began to go deeper, it all started to make sense. The fragments of my conditioned patterns that had been keeping me from seeing my life clearly, were playing out right in front of my eyes though the actions of this horse. He helped me to see, without judgment, what I needed to do differently to change the unhealthy dynamics in my life. How did he know? How was he so gracefully reflecting the experience that I had been living?

The Effects of Being Out of Balance

Because I had learned to value my intellect and was never taught how to listen to my emotions or inner wisdom, I did not pay attention to the red flags signaling that my life was out of balance.

I also realized that without learning the subtlety of simultaneous awareness in connection to others, relationships could become a painful experience. I had an epiphany when I began to understand all that the horse had shown me, and how that related to my life at home and at work. This was key in realizing why many of our experiences in life and business end up falling short of what we most desire.

Having spent most of my adult life working with Fortune 500 companies, I felt a great sense of sadness for what we, as a culture, had been missing. The lack of personal awareness was causing ripple effects of dysfunction through individuals, families and organizations. In many cases, people resorted to acquiescence, or conversely, dominance, to compensate for personal imbalance.

A New Beginning

What I learned was not about the horses, it was about me, and the way I had been living my life. This equine dance of biofeedback was extraordinary. It was exquisite personal guidance at the most intimate level, something I never could have learned from a book or a lecture. From that point forward, my new direction was born. Up to that point, my life had been the sum of all that I had learned and this had offered the crucial missing piece that I needed to move forward. I was willing to let go of the things that needed to change, thus I was opened to a new life-breath of inspiration, one that helped me to fulfill my greatest dream so far... Epona Ridge.

My journey started when a book landed in my lap. Now this chapter is in yours, and you have opened to this page...

Barbara Alexander is the Founder and Director of Epona Ridge, Teacher and Leading Innovator of Equine Experiential Learning and Coaching for Advanced Human Development. Epona Ridge, a sanctuary retreat center for inspiration, is located in Asheville, North Carolina and offers life and career support, Reiki certification, facilitator training, individual workshops and retreats incorporating the teachings of Abraham – Hicks and the Law of Allowing. For more information see: *www.EponaRidge.com* and *www.BarbaraAlexanderCoachingWithHorses.com*

ELIMINATE CLUTTER, CHAOS AND CONFUSION WITH 2 PRINCIPLES, 3 RULES AND 10 STEPS

by Susan Wagers

I t's not the tragedies that kill us, it's the messes," says Dorothy Parker.

So many things to do, so little time! Does this phrase describe your personal and professional life? You are definitely not alone if you are feeling a need to simplify and organize your life.

A recent survey revealed:

- 42% of adults report that too often they feel "life is a treadmill and I can't get off." (Think of Astro, the family's pet dog in the cartoon, The Jetson's.)

- 78% of adults say they wish they had more time to "stop and smell the roses."

- 58% believe technological advances have given them more time. But they are using old habits with new technology; we need new habits.

- 81% of people consider themselves organized, *YET—*

- 83% say getting more organized is one of their top goals.

If you are feeling a need to simplify and organize your life, you are definitely not alone

- Every day, the average person spends between 20 minutes and two hours looking for things.

- Americans waste more than 9 million hours each year looking for lost and misplaced articles.
- We are bombarded with information from every direction, with 150,000 books and 10,000 periodicals published each year in the USA.

Imagine YOUR life…

- When you are more productive and feel more effective.
- When your creativity is unleashed and you experience freedom because you are organized.
- When you learn it is possible for an organized and balanced life to be your reality.

Organizing *is not* about neatness or making things tidy. (Though neat people work with us, too!) It is not about being perfect or being rigid. (If you are, we love you anyway.) Organization *is* about being able to find what you want, when you want, and getting things done.

Eliminating clutter, chaos and confusion is your first step to creating a life *In Balance – In Sync*. People who are successful share a common secret. They know that to get ahead they must plan, set priorities and always follow through. As a result, they develop systems that work for them. With a system in place, you will never lose, never misplace, and never forget again because you will have a defined structure and process to follow and fall back on again when life gets crazy.

The primary reason for disorganization is *indecision*—What do I do with this? Where do I put this? We've identified the three main organizational challenges—Clutter, Chaos, and Confusion caused by imbalances in time, paper, and space management.

Clutter creates Confusion, which then creates Chaos.

Knowing just a few shortcuts and simple "truths about organizing" can certainly make every day easier and a lot more fun.

Time Management is Really Self-management

Time, as defined by *Webster*, is the measured or measurable period during which an action, process, or condition exits or continues; the point or period when something occurs.

We all have the same amount of time:

- 24 hours per day
- 168 hours per week
- 744 hours per month

Do you know the Law of the Slight Edge? Here's what it says:

If you would better use just one hour a day, 365 days a year (weekend, too), your yield would be an additional 45 – 8 hour days. That's 1 ½ months!

According to an association of professional organizers, you spend six weeks a year looking for stuff. Yikes! That's 42 days of every year spent looking for stuff?

Here's the point...

If you better used one hour per day and never had to look for stuff, you could possibly recapture three months of time.

No way, you say! Oh yea, its' possible but first you have to commit to making changes and a baby with a wet diaper is the only human I know who likes change.

Beware and be aware of these Timewasters:

- Procrastination
- Inability to say "NO"
- Indecision
- Looking for lost items
- Shuffling papers
- Perfectionism

As Robert Cannan, a corporate consultant, reminds us:

"Time management is really Self-management."

The Paper Chase

You need to establish one place which is designated as the collection area. This is a necessity whether you like it or not. It doesn't matter if you have an official "IN" Box or Basket or the dining room table, the key here is one designated collection area.

Everyone puts "stuff" in here for you. When you empty it you establish credibility with others. They know you saw what they brought you and are working on it. Empty it every time you are there. Make sure it is empty before you leave.

Make your paper processing system as simple as possible to avoid paralysis by analysis. The easiest one I know to stick with is the 4-D System:

Do • Dump • Delegate • Delay

There's so much to read! Although reading is an action, any paper that requires more than five or ten minutes of reading time should be handled through your system. Process short articles as you would any other papers, but set aside a separate box or shelf space for lengthy reports, trade journals, and other publications.

Sort all incoming papers through your paper processing system, moving them from your desk to wastebasket, reference folder, action box or tickler file, file cabinet, or reading stack.

Space Management

Four critical questions:

1. Are the things I need most, closest to where I work?
2. Is my desk really a work surface or a file cabinet?
3. Are the files closest to me the ones I work the most out of?
4. Do I retrieve things the first time I look for them?

Divide your work area into a:

Primary desk

Support areas – other work surfaces

Personal files

Special Organizing Hints:

- Place like things together.
- Label notebooks and storage boxes clearly and on all four sides.
- Everything that stays close to you must earn its keep.
- Right hand people—phone to the left; Left hand people—phone to the right.
- Put extra pens and pencils away and off your desk—you can only write with one at a time.
- Designate a place where all incoming papers begin.
- Keep only those items you use daily on top of your desk. Everything else finds a home in a drawer.

Here's the point...

2 Principles

1. It takes longer than you think to complete any task.
2. It will get worse before it gets better.

3 Rules

1. Resist being a pack rat—replacing it is probably easier than storing it. Ask yourself: "What's the worse thing that can happen if I get rid of ......?"

2. Stop hoarding junk. Old newspaper clippings, pens that don't write, things that have no home. Everything has a place and everything is in its place. If homeless, give it a home or get rid of it.

3. Make an even exchange. Something new in—something old out. This is true for everything and everyone.

10 daily action steps to simplify your life because Clutter creates Confusion, which then creates Chaos.

- Keep rooms clutter-free.

- Everything **has** its place – Everything **is in** its place.

- File and re-file immediately.

- All pending work is in one or two files/drawers.

- Tickler file is completed.

- Update your calendar(s).

- Set your priorities and know where you are going.

- Pick it up, don't pass it up, and put it away.

- Do it when you think of it.

- Don't write long letters.

The cycle always goes on but now you have the tools to gain and maintain control.

We all have the same amount of time. Organizing comes back to you in seconds, seconds to minutes and minutes to create extra hours per day. Organizing will help you produce better work, become more productive, be a better role model, and have more fun every day.

Here's the final point...

- Don't attempt everything at once or in one day.

- Start with one area.

- See and feel some accomplishment before moving on to the next area.

- Remember—organization is a system that needs to incorporate a habit and a tool.

- The habit takes time—experts say you need 21 days to break and/or create a new habit.

Susan Wagers is the owner of multiple businesses and is a Workflow Productivity Coach with over 20 years experience in creating environments rooted in discipline, organization, strong routine and persistent activity. She is an award winning business woman, public speaker, author of nationally published articles, and four life-planning books. Her publications include checklists and simple tools to create a life In Balance-In Sync! with your priorities and goals.

http://ProductivityCoachSusan.com/sq

MAKE LIFE YOUR BUSINESS

by Cindy Melton

L ife is not stagnant. It flows through hopes, dreams and passions. You are conducting the orchestra and influencing the movement and precious moments of your life. The life that you desire may yet be waiting to be discovered. You are the creator and author of your own stories and experiences as expressed in your own handwriting. If you are not happy with the rhythm of your life it's never too late to design a new blueprint, create a new symphony, write the chapter you long to experience and make life your business.

No matter how we try to plan each moment in life something out of the ordinary, unforeseen or unpredictable happens. Most likely these events do not present themselves within the schedule we created. Falling in love, declining health, the birth of a new baby, a diagnosis of cancer, a home foreclosed, a war commenced, life earnings lost in the stock market, or an unexpected death are all situations and challenges that may present themselves. When life happens it is important not to look solely at the circumstances but to look at what you learn and thus gain from them. This can be a blessing in disguise. Sometimes, in order to get a clearer picture and to uncover what truly matters, we are required to look through a different set of lenses and form a different viewpoint. One thing is certain. Life is happening in this very moment.

I know many people who are aching to be and achieve more in life, and have no idea where to begin. We spend our lives planning for education, a degree, a career choice, and a job to make money. Often, this results in living paycheck-to-paycheck, working at a job that requires the majority of our time, zapping our energy, until there is nothing more of us left to give. Relationships fall apart, family values disintegrate, and crime and homelessness become prevalent. As a nation, there is no value or honor placed on a person's life, his or her body, God, the family unit, personal health, relationships, or job security. There are a lot of people simply waiting on the sidelines for someone else to fix their and the world's problems.

Therein lies the real challenge for answers to life problems. Solutions begin with us. There is power and strength in numbers. We have a wealth of knowledge, experience and technology—resources available to anyone who wants to create a better life for themselves. To be successful and make a significant difference in all areas of life you need to maximize your moments with true value and be present in each moment.

Give yourself permission to dream and dream big. Perhaps your dream is to climb Mt. Everest, learn to play the guitar or discover a cure for cancer. Perhaps it is to become a better parent, improve yourself or give God permission to bless your life. It is hard for some to believe but in this very moment, God is present, watching over us. All the obstacles in the world can be recognized to be the greatest opportunities to create unique solutions that will benefit mankind and the world, and honor God.

Where has God placed you and why has He placed you there? Is there one person in your family that you can invest your time, love, energy, and the resources that you have in? Who can you impact in a positive and constructive manner? A vision, dream, or solution begins in the heart and in the imagination. When we celebrate the small beginnings of new life creations, a little becomes a lot. The momentum created can move mountains, metaphorically speaking, and miracles happen in the least expected places.

If your dream is to just to make a lot of money quick, and you go from one scheme to another to get rich, those trial and errors will not work. You have to give in order to receive. You need to cherish and nurture what is in your heart as passionately as you would pursue your monetary ambition. If you have a dream, write it down, make it tangible. It becomes your unique and inspiring vision. See it, touch it, feel it, breathe it. Embrace your vision fully and make it real. Let it become the life of your creation based on your values. Live it!

Many people live in one of two phases in life, the past or the future. It's easier to keep looking in the rear view mirror, focusing on what was, than to step out in faith to follow a maybe. Sometimes, that's all we have, a simple maybe, a glimmer of hope, a spark of passion, and it makes all the difference encouraging us to move forward into a life of creation.

We need to live life in constant expectation that good things will happen all around us. We need to see that good things are happening. Support is and will always be there for every step we take in the direction of our dreams but we often don't hear it, see it, or believe in the vision. "Why do some of us live life this way?" Mostly because we do not understand the need for a strategic plan necessary in order to leave the past, and step forward into a life that we author.

Some people choose to stay in the past, which never allows them to experience a life of creation, as life is meant to be. Others dream about the future but choose to ignore the moment because the busyness of life gets in the way. What they lack is a vision that cherishes every moment by its very design. Has anyone ever said to you, "I'll believe it when I see it"?

In my coaching practice I often discuss a story, which takes place between two men, and illustrates my point further. My grandmother shared this story with me when I was a child. The story is about how one man who had faith in his vision and another who would not believe in it because he couldn't see it.

Walter asked his friend to go for a ride with him out to the country. They drove off the beaten road onto a large space of land. A few horses were grazing, and some old shacks were barely standing on the property. Walter stopped the car, got out, and described the wonderful things he was going to build on this spot.

His friend looked at the barren property and thought to himself, "Who is going to drive this far out into the country?" Walter explained to his friend, "I can handle this myself, but it will take all my money. There will be hotels, and restaurants on this property for families to spend their vacations at." He continued, "I want you to have the first chance at purchasing the surrounding land because in the future it will increase in value."

This is the story of how Walt Disney began his journey to realize his vision for Disneyland. His friend, Art Linkletter, on the other hand, turned down the opportunity to invest in what would become, as Disney had envisioned, a highly valued property.

Creating a Vision is like going for an inspiring walk in a beautiful lush setting. One step at a time, you begin to imagine yourself living the life of your dreams and you begin to see a vivid picture of your amazing life unfolding. When you claim it, it becomes yours. This might be the very impetus needed to create highly valuable, significant and meaningful solutions, for the future generations, which God has designed for you to achieve.

The disappointments of the past that you hold onto can prevent you from creating the life your dreams. We surround ourselves with things large and small, things that give us temporary pleasure, things that are filled with hidden memories and some that are treasured. What is it that we are hoping for when we fill our hearts and homes with stuff? When stuff fills up space in your life it's impossible to have a feeling of wellness or peace. Everything becomes a disorganized mess. Our life becomes cluttered.

Our decisions reflect our values and how we choose to live our lives. Does your day timer reflect your highest priorities? That which is truly important to you? Is there quality time allotted to honor and interact with those you love the most? Is there time planned for building meaningful relationships? OR, does your calendar reflect a schedule of all work and no play. Decide what your priorities are. Cherish and nurture your life and do not place too much value on mindless and meaningless activities, or on the physical "stuff" that fills homes, feeds greed and often causes an imbalance and unnecessary pressures, which in turn destroy lives.

Everyone goes through life with stresses, problems, and challenges. We don't just sit there. Life moves on. If you find yourself living life on the edge or feeling that the game of life is suffocating you, there is a way to move forward and get past these limitations. Simply stop, slow down, breathe deeply, and press the delete button. Decide to change to a new and improved direction. Stretch a little bit higher and reach out beyond your comfort zone. Create and expand a vision unique to you in alignment with your heartfelt values. There is no need to worry about how you will accomplish it at this point. Free your imagination and open your heart to express its deepest desires and the true and authentic passions within you.

If you want something you've never had before, do things you've never done before. Don't feel that you have to settle for mediocrity. That is a self imposed myth and limiting belief. Choose instead to create that brand new and inspiring vision of you living an amazing life based on and in alignment with what is truly important to you. Grasp onto it. Commit to it! Keep it vivid in your mind's eye and in the depths of your heart at all times. Let it be your daily motivation. Then go make it happen!

This will keep you focused thus enabling you to target your time, energy and resources towards creating the life of your dreams in real time. Grow forward to meet and exceed all your expectations, keeping your clear and exciting vision fresh and alive. The desires of your heart are carved in your own handwriting, this very moment. Take charge of yourself and make the only life you have your business!

Nurture it! Value it! Make it worthwhile! Feel blessed! Be grateful! Your precious life is God's most generous gift! Be worthy and share your unique essence in every great and honorable way!

Cindy Melton has twenty-five years experience Coaching people to celebrate the little things of Every Day Life. She inspires people to look within their heart and soul to take personal responsibility to choose to live Life in Abundance. In group speaking about the HealthyEdge, she gives you simple tools to gain insights and heartfelt wisdom for achieving optimal Health, Success living, and a Prosperous God Realized Life. Cindy is also the CoFounder of TEAM-BoomerPreneurs, whose heart and vision is nurturing the Every Day Entrepreneur.

Visit *http:www.ImpactHealthToday.com/sq* or to learn about Every Day Life Tips, Hope and Healing, visit NurtureYourLife Blog at *http://NurtureYourLifeblogspot.com*

Make Life Easier

by Jeffrey A. Betman, PhD

For most people, life just keeps getting harder and more complex. Wouldn't it be nice if life got easier? Below are seven secrets proven to work if you apply them. Your life will get easier. My clients have lowered their stress levels, worked less, felt happier and more confident. They walk tall with a sense of purpose.

We aren't just talking about reading these secrets and saying to yourself "I know that." No, we are talking about making "these" part of your life. Like brushing your teeth, these secrets will pay off in the short term and over the course of your life. The goal here is to make your life easier.

Secret #1: Having a purpose makes life easier.

We are all overloaded with too much to do and seemingly too little time. Without a purpose, you are rudderless at sea. You will be banged and pushed about by every current and wave coming at you. Without purpose you will feel overwhelmed and out of time. Your purpose guides your life and how you spend your time. This is the secret from which all others flow.

It is much easier to say yes or no to various meetings and activities if you filter them through your purpose. Otherwise, you are destined for overwhelm, attending countless time-wasting meetings, and will continue to get sucked into doing stupid things your really don't want to do. Imagine giant invisible vacuums sucking your time, energy, and spirit right out of you. Gross!

Recent research reveals people live longer when they have a purpose. Your purpose does not have to be monumental. It can be anything from learning to relax to being a better spouse to volunteering at the local library. Having a purpose is the critical element here.

I had a client recently who came to me overwhelmed, exhausted, stressed and ready to quit her job. Once she remembered her purpose of supporting her husband and expertly managing her employees, she relaxed and began having fun again.

Secret #2: Awake with gratitude and attract great gifts.

Your choice: awake negative, awake neutral or awake with gratitude. Gratitude sets you on a specific path to the exclusion of all others. Starting your day with this mindset opens you up to receive everything coming your way or even that is in your vicinity. Be grateful for what you've *had*, what you have *now*, and what you *will* have (this last point courtesy of the great motivational speaker Mike Wickett).

Future gratitude is the term I use for the great things coming into your life that haven't arrived yet. Think of it as priming the gratitude pump to make your life easier. Gratitude seems to ward off negativity, stress, worry, anger, and anxiety according to Wallace D. Wattles in *The Science of Getting Rich*. He goes on to state, "the grateful mind is constantly fixed upon the best."

The grateful mind cannot simultaneously be grateful and negative (e.g. worried or anxious). Gratitude trumps negativity.

Secret #3: This would be a good time to start swimming.

Seems to me that most people are doing everything they can just to tread water. By the time work and daily activities are completed, there is no time for making progress on goals. But ask yourself: do you want to just tread water or actually swim? Treading water takes tons of energy and soon you will sink into a "life of quiet desperation."

Growing and improving yourself is about stretching and moving toward goals. The most difficult step is starting, which takes the most amount of energy. Think about moving a boulder forward. You would stress and strain at first, but then the boulder would start rolling and your energy output would be less due to momentum. Moving forward gives you momentum.

Keep pushing that boulder everyday. It gets easier from the twin powers of habit and momentum. You are proactive, not reactive. This makes life easier as you are in control and can handle life when the waves start rolling in, which they always do.

Yes, I am mixing metaphors of swimming and boulders here. But, at least you aren't underwater pushing boulders around.

Secret #4: Don't be a slob. Your mother told you to clean up your room, now clean up your life.

How can you reach your full potential while fermenting in disorganization? If you can't see the floor, you are a slob. If you've ever been late to work because you couldn't find your keys, your life is messy. If you spend more than two minutes retrieving a file, you are disorganized. Life is harder when you are disorganized.

Disorganization robs you of calmness and tranquility; leads to frustration, aggravation and stress. Most visits to physicians are stress related. We are not talking house beautiful or office beautiful here. We are talking reasonable organization given your circumstances. Part of the problem is we all have too much stuff, which gives us more to organize. Less stuff equals less to organize and search through. Order brings calmness. Order reduces stress and makes life easier.

Secret #5: Work at your prime time.

This may seem like a no-brainer, but many people don't work at their primetime or don't even know when it is. Primetime is that time during the day when you are at your best, most creative, and in the zone. Everybody has different prime times; what matters is to know yours and work accordingly. When have you felt "on fire"? When was that during the day?

Match your primetime with your most important tasks that require your undivided attention. This is not the time to multi-task. Save the less important, more routine tasks for your nonprime periods during the day. My primetime is in the morning so I do my heavy brainwork early in the day such as writing reports, planning projects, or mind mapping solutions to projects. I save tasks such as answering emails and opening junk mail for the afternoon. They still require brainpower, but less.

Secret #6: Become Un-balanced.

Don't you hate it when people tell you to get your life in balance? Who are they kidding? Maybe it is a great ideal to shoot for, but maybe it is unachievable and puts too much stress on you to attempt achieving it.

I contend that *there is no difference between work and life. It is all life.* Creating a false line between work and the rest of your life implies they are separate, and then people go about trying to balance them out. Wouldn't it be much easier to give up the distinction, and just live your life?

Remember, you are balancing your life over time, not every minute. Certain parts of your life will demand more attention than others at any given point in time. Your life will be unbalanced. Trying to maintain balance while appropriately focusing on one or two areas of life will drive you up the wall. It is not possible, so give it up.

Secret #7: Everybody knows your secret.

That is because they most likely have the same secret. One that they feel they are alone with, but in reality share with most of their friends and family. They feel inadequate, not good enough, even like an impostor. They typically feel like this their entire life. The problem is this secret affects everything in your life. It affects every decision you make, how you perceive events around you and how you think, walk and talk.

Most people miss out on their true gifts. They have almost no patience with themselves; compared to the patience they show others, even complete strangers. Living this secret costs you. It holds you back. It causes you to hesitate rather than jump at opportunities. It causes you to stay in your comfort zone too long to the point of living a life of "quiet desperation."

Living an easier life takes some effort, discipline and persistence. It is more about cutting stuff out rather than adding stuff in. Coming at life from a different perspective than most people. Action steps for these secrets are available on my website.

Jeffrey A. Betman, Ph.D. is a psychologist, author, and life coach helping people toward the easy life. He has over 23 years of experience as a clinical psychologist and more recently as a life coach working with clients from all over the world. For more information about Dr. Betman and specific action steps for each of these seven secrets go to *www.LifeIsEasyCoaching.com*

GOT PROBLEMS AT WORK? BE GRATEFUL!

by Jeffrey A. Betman, PhD

Don't play the blame game... play the solution game instead!

Here's the scene – a meeting room on any given day at any given work place. A group of individuals are excitedly discussing the problem du jour. This group of critics is so wrapped up in the problem that they're failing to look to for the solution. Ever been in this room? What a waste of time and energy! *Don't* let this happen to you.

Let me ask you a few questions. Who gets the promotion, the person finding the most problems? Or the employee who comes up with most solutions? In bad times, who has the most job security; the blame assigners or the problem solvers? Who gets paid the most money the "inspectors" who find problems or the "designers" that invent the solutions? I'm sure you get my point. Let me show you how to avoid wasting time and energy playing the blame game and play the solution game instead.

First, realize that problems are a normal, natural and an unavoidable fact of life. One description of work could be "one continuous succession of problems." As long as you're alive, they are never ending. Problems only vary in size and importance. This is great news for problem solvers like you and me!

Second, the only part of this "succession of problems" that you control is your attitude. You alone choose the manner in which you approach each problem as it arises. Unfortunately most people are simply overwhelmed by problems. They talk continually about who is to blame, why the problem occurred and the possible damage or cost. The longer this blame game goes on, the more animated the discussion becomes and the more likely it is that someone becomes angry.

Anger activates the ancient "fight or flight" response in our bodies. This pump of adrenaline can make us irrational. Bad decisions are made by people who are *not rational*. While angry, most of us have said or done things that we would move heaven and earth to reverse. I certainly have. Let's face it the madder we get, the dumber we act. Anger just doesn't solve problems.

The Solutions Game

Be grateful for your problems! Make it *your job* to be solution oriented. You should concentrate all your energies on what can be done to solve the problem. Solution oriented people are the most valuable people in any organization. They are positive and constructive. They concentrate on solutions to what has already occurred and cannot be changed.

Here's the tool that allows you can to change your attitude from negative and worried to positive and constructive in a single moment. Switch your thoughts off of the problem and onto the solution. Simple—yes? You just stop asking or worrying about who did what and who's to blame. Instead you ask the questions, "What do we do now?" and "What's the solution?"

Do not make the critical error of <u>thinking in reverse</u>. Unfortunately, life has no "do over" button. Do not live in the past. Look at the past only long enough to identify the root causes of our problem. Gratefully live and work on the solution today, while concentrating on moving forward. Know that the results of an effectively executed solution lie in the future.

Enlist all the resources at your disposal. This is a place where role models, mentors and coaches can help. As you face challenges, a first step is to act as if. Meaning, you act **as if** you are someone who can solve the problem even if you need to pretend to be one of your role models at first. Now that you're confident you're the right person to find the solution, or at least know how to act like one, take action!

Start asking questions. Ask "Who knows more about this problem (process, product, personnel issue, etc) than me?" "Who's the expert in this area?" Then visit that person, and ask for help. Ask "When have I encountered something like this before?" Refer to the solution that was used for that similar problem and see if it fits. If not, see if you can modify the solution in some way. If the previous fix still doesn't work *fine*, just keep taking self-directed, positive, *on-purpose* action towards finding a solution.

Your mind is designed in such a way that the more you focus on solutions, the more solutions you will find. This is why "brain storming" is a popular and effective technique. The more you think and talk about solutions, the faster and easier you will come up with even better solutions. You will actually become more creative and competent at solving problems, dealing with difficulties, achieving goals and getting key results as you discipline yourself to focus increasingly on the positive, constructive steps you can take.

Concentrate On "Win – Win" Outcomes

As Dr. Stephen Covey said, "Think 'Win-Win' isn't about being *nice*, nor is it a quick-fix technique. It is a character-based code for human interaction and collaboration." Your problem solving must find solutions that allow everyone to walk away with a win. For example, selling products below cost makes no sense if the company goes out of business. Yet charging high prices does the company no good if there are no customers willing to pay the price. The end result in either case is customers who don't have the use of the product and a company that is broke.

Success in your career will be largely determined by your ability to solve the problems that you encounter. As you get better at solving problems, you'll be given bigger problems to solve. This is a good thing! Be grateful! The bigger and more costly the problems you solve, the more money you will be paid, the more power you will have and the higher the position you will attain. As you demonstrate that you can solve your current problems, you will be promoted to dealing with problems of greater complexity and importance.

Always choose to play the solution game. Make yourself the person that people bring their problems to because you always have good ideas about how to solve them. Concentrating on the solution game allows you to think more effectively and generate better solutions. Be grateful for your problems. They allow you to play the solution game that puts your entire life and career on the fast track toward being paid more and promoted faster.

Bill Becker has worked in numerous different businesses, often starting at the bottom and moving through the management ranks. Bill is a speaker, trainer, manager and coach. In his mid-20s, he became a construction supervisor and began climbing up through the business world. He is a graduate of the College at Oswego with B.S. in Vocational/Technical Education. Today, Bill's focus is on helping others overcome their limiting beliefs through success coaching. His mission is to provide you with the tools and tips you need to create the life you love! For additional information on his coaching programs visit his website at: *coachbillbecker.com/sq*

SIMPLE STEPS TO THRIVING BEYOND PAIN:

Pull Weeds, Plant Flowers!

by Malcolm F. Dayton, LPC, CHt

I f you are old enough to walk and talk, then you clearly understand a fundamental truth: With living comes pain—physical, emotional, and relationship pain, fear, anxiety, depression, grief, trauma. Pain simply is; but not all pain must result in suffering.

Perhaps you have known depths of pain so intense that something MUST change... NOW! Whether your pain is chronic and physical or better described as mental-emotional, the steps for you to thrive beyond pain now are similar.

In this section, you will:

- Discover why chronic physical pain and mental-emotional pain can be addressed with similar skills;

- Experience a fundamental transformation in how you perceive and process pain—to thrive beyond pain; and

- Learn to live free beyond your history of pain and suffering.

Bold claims, I know; but for over 25 years, I have been blessed to coach and counsel hundreds of individuals, couples and families in living beyond pain and suffering. I have also travelled my own path of chronic pain, depression, and loss (traversing multiple sclerosis, immune deficiency and asthma); and I can assure you, if you take the steps I outline here, you will forever transform your experience of pain!

In my case, I went from living daily with prescribed narcotics and anti-seizure medications to being able to live more fully (in awe), with **no** prescribed pain medications and only occasional ibuprofen. These strategies work... if you work them; and like any skill set, they require playful practice.

We will approach the skills associated with thriving beyond pain in the same way we approach cultivating a beautiful garden. First, we pull weeds; then, we plant flowers. From that point on, we only have to nourish and maintain our lovely creation. To begin, however, we must...

Pull the Weeds of Limiting Goals

Each coaching relationship begins by laying out your desired results. It may seem counter-intuitive, but we will NOT set out to relieve or alleviate pain. In fact, seeking pain relief is the first "weed" we must eliminate.

If we seek "pain relief", we are effectively beginning from a place that denies our experience—the pain. In addition, it sets us on a path of seeking the "absence of an experience," much like wanting "out of a job" rather than focusing on the passionate work you desire to move toward.

In my personal and professional experience, "moving away from" goals typically solve very little. Because moving-away-from goals are driven by solutions outside you, they become effectively disempowering. Instead, we must...

Plant the Flowers of Empowering Vision

Create clear, enticing, moving-toward-goals built with emotion and meaning around the activities you value highly and desire to carry out again; goals that drive your passion from within; goals that empower you and motivate you to consistently access and develop rediscovered resources within (those abilities you have had since infancy, but have remained dormant for years, perhaps decades). Next...

Pull the Weeds of Separating Within

You must experientially come to terms with a fundamental fact— "body" and "mind" are not separate. We are a living, breathing, whole bodymind experience. Pain does not occur in "body"; nor does it occur in "mind." Pain occurs in you, as you, through you. You are a unified experience of bodymind.

Therefore, you cannot simply separate solutions into "body" remedies and "mind" remedies. You must experience self-as-whole; otherwise, you risk merely treating symptoms and masking pain (resulting in still more intense, prolonged pain). Instead, you will...

Plant the Flowers of Bodyminding

The key transformative skill for you to experience is awareness of the one-you who experiences! You are not merely the sum of cells and organs: You are awareness witnessing the entire bodymind experiencing now.

This is so important that I will repeat it: The key transformative skill for you to experience is awareness of self-as-whole: You are awareness witnessing the bodymind experience occurring in every cell, every moment.

In short, you are not "a bodymind"; rather you "bodymind" moment-to-moment, from the cells of the scalp to those at the tips of the toes. Each day, take time to luxuriate in that flowering bodymind awareness.

This shift in perspective is so essential if you are to successfully thrive beyond pain! It is much like those pictures made of colored dots: You search for meaning in the collage, when suddenly... a 3-D picture pops out into awareness (and your experience is forever changed).

Bodyminding-beyond-the-pain is much the same process: Awful pain resides in sensing self in a piecemeal fashion. AweFulliving™ occurs in the whole, vibrant experience of this moment "now" requiring you to also...

Pull the Weeds of Possessing

A steady, debilitating companion of intense pain comes when we "own" the experience. Similar to "separating within," experiencing "my" pain or commiserating about "my" pain further entrenches and intensifies the pain experience.

Just as you must develop new bodymind sensitivity, you must also develop an entirely new approach to your thoughts and language concerning pain. Every time you focus on "my" pain, you put yourself right back into a limiting body experience. Instead, you must...

Plant the Flowers of Paining

Be very clear that pain is not "you" nor is it a thing inside that you own. It is an **experience-of-living**. Certainly it can be extremely discomforting, but experience constantly changes, morphs and evolves.

I teach clients "to pain" (a verb), rather than to have "pain" (a noun): To pain is to experience sensations. So, one of the secrets to thriving beyond pain is to witness that sensing—a skill you have employed many times before.

Recall how you played as a child: In much the same way, you can shape experience moment-to-moment. Imagine being some distance from yourself; just watching, observing yourself as you pain away. As you fully give into this witnessing, you may discover that different cells of bodymind reflect different colors, different shapes in various sizes, different temperatures, even various aromas and tastes.

You may decide to play with these perceptions by intentionally changing those shapes, colors, size, etc. You may even imagine bodymind melting into a puddle of relaxation... now...

Then suddenly (just as with the dots), rather than being in awful pain, you realize you can play longer and longer in whole new dimensions of AweFulliving™. From just such awareness, pain becomes the canvas on which you create the watercolor plan for your lovely garden; and then, you begin to...

Pull the Weeds of Story-Telling

Particularly with pain of long duration and multiple, unsuccessful attempts at relief, we naturally begin to develop a "story" of who-I-am—one that makes sense of the suffering. The problem is we easily begin to identify with that story; and as we do, we subtly align more and more with that limiting misrepresentation of self.

Just as with "owning" the pain, we actually become identified with more pain; so much so, that some will actually fight to maintain their distorted identity. We get into arguments with self and others about deserving (or not) this painful experience. We stumble into new-age-guilt that comes with the western emphasis on cause-and-effect. We become "victim" in this tale of woe, and can readily spiral into abject fear and hopelessness. All of which more deeply entrenches the pain. Instead, we must simply...

Plant Flowers!

As with bodyminding and paining, you must be willing to appreciate and to experience your fullness now. You are more than the pain-filled experiences you have had up to now.

You are still unique, special and a beautiful flower just as you are—nothing needs to change for you to own that, except your willingness to allow yourself to be the flowering gift.

Imagine yourself as you were when just-born. Take a long, deep, loving look at the beautiful infant... Yes, you have grown older and are shaped differently now, but you remain the precious flower born to this planet. Pull the weeds of your old story. Allow yourself to be the beauty you are for all to enjoy. If you must believe a story, believe this story, own this story every day and in every moment:

56

Malcolm Dayton is a Licensed Counselor with over two decades serving individuals and families facing chronic illness. He is also certified in MindBody Medicine and Hypnotherapy. Malcolm's AweFulliving™ Coaching Program is unique; combining his personal success in thriving beyond lifelong illness with his clinical success in coaching others to thrive beyond chronic illness. Malcolm walks his coaching! Malcolm's mission is to Coach You WELL! To find out more go to
http://CoachingSelfHealing.com/sq

THE BALANCING ACT OF WORK AND LIFE

by Joseph (Joe) Becwar

"**O**ur lives are a mixture of different roles. Most of us are doing the best we can to find whatever the right balance is... For me, that balance is family, work, and service." H.R Clinton

For most people life is a balance between family, friends, and work. The roles we play in each situation can seem to be extremely different. However, it is the priority we give to each one that makes up how we choose to live our lives or how our lives become defined. As humans we are not able to separate what is going on in our professional lives from our personal lives or vice versa. We can dedicate ourselves to achieving success or perfection at one or the other but we cannot omit the impact that either one has on another aspect of our life and the lives of those around us. Our lives are a balancing act of skills, knowledge, trust, acceptance, rejection, forgiveness, money, peace of mind, happiness, and commitment to ourselves both personally and professionally,

To see how we balance our lives, we need to look at two key areas: work and personal life. Once we do so we can address how to create a more balanced, fuller life.

So many times, people say that they really aren't happy at work. Even if they don't want to be in the field they are in, they either continue to put in long hours and commit themselves to striving for success, or decide to just "get by" with their minimal efforts. They are not energized by or passionate about what they are doing and maintain a commitment to their work only because it is expected of them for many reasons: good pay, degree, security.

Look at what makes you happy at work. Is it being the person everyone depends on? Do you feel needed? Now, look at your personal life. Are the same attributes visible here? Are you needed? Do you feel needed? Do you socialize outside of the workplace? It is important also to feel a connection with people away from your working environment. If not, you may need to look deeper at the balance in your life.

How do your coworkers balance their lives? Not everyone is connected to a computer or blackberry. Not everyone works weekends or during vacations. The key to balance is that you are able to let go of some of the control and possible fear that is associated with not being available 24/7.

Many times people feel they are the only ones who can answer questions or need to be in the office in case something comes up. In business, this is what is called the "fixer"—the person who wants to put out fires instead of allowing others to learn to deal with issues when you are not around. What the "fixer" ends up creating are excuses for not fully committing to personal growth and living the other part of their lives. In essence, they have chosen not allow self-growth and relaxation outside of how they have defined their life by their job.

Do you constantly check your email or blackberry at work and home? What is it you are looking for when you check it so much? Start by turning off your inbox updates. Check your email throughout the day but don't switch back and forth. No one can really "multitask." All you are doing is refocusing your attention to something else, requiring you to then refocus to complete the task you turned away from.

Now let's look at some life issues.

Taking personal time to spend with coworkers can be important. However, it can also take over your life and significantly reduce the time you spend with family and friends. It is easy to slip into a routine of going out after work or only socializing with coworkers. When you limit your circle of whom you socialize with to coworkers, it can easily control of your free time.

You can get drawn into a "snowball effect." When you are not able to see yourself as having a life outside of your work you start to see your coworkers as a bigger part of your life. You live within your comfort zone, not having to work on other personal relationships. This can even lead to having more than platonic feelings for those you work with. In extreme cases, some people let workplace relationships replace outside friendships entirely.

The danger to living like this is that if your support system disappears or changes dramatically, it leaves you feeling as if you have no one to turn to. Many times people either don't have someone to turn to outside of work, or only reach out to friends and family when things are bad. If you do this what kind of person are you seen as by those friends or family, other than someone who is always negative? For this reason alone, it is important to have someone outside your work circle to share both your successes and failures. When we nurture your relationships with family and friends we build a support system that is not based on work but on personality and love. It is important to work toward balancing your actions. To be able to receive we must give of ourselves.

Work life balance doesn't only apply to those with a significant other or children. The reason we need time to yourselves or your personal life is to recharge. It can come in many different forms—friendships, volunteering, mentoring or making time for recreation, sports, or doing something you are passionate about. We all need down time to do things we enjoy and to bring joy into our lives. If we never stop to see and participate in all the possibilities life has to offer we are never able to grow towards living a balanced life.

Here is one way to get started achieving balance in your life.

Make a list of you top priorities, numbering no more than five. Then really take some time to think about prioritizing them in order of importance. If you could give all your attention to one thing in life, what would it be? Then add the subsequent things in the same way, asking what is the one thing you would focus on if you achieved the first (second, and third etc.) priority. Remember to list what you **want** them to be, not what they **should** be.

The result will be a list of your top priorities and may include: relationship, kids, money, career, leisure time for hobbies, travel etc.

Whatever you choose as priorities, make a commitment to give each a specific amount of time and attention, and only focus on one priority at a time. When you need to focus on work give it your full attention. When you need to spend time with your partner then commit to giving that person your full attention. This may seem counterintuitive to achieving balance, but it is not. By having a list of priorities that recognizes other important aspects of your life, and then focusing on one at a time, you are inherently achieving greater balance.

Start letting go of any commitments and pursuits that do not make your top-five list, because unnecessary activities keep you away from the things that matter to you most.

You would probably think twice before skipping out on work, a parent-teacher conference, or a doctor's appointment. Your private time deserves the same respect. If work consistently interferes with your personal time, demonstrate that you can deliver the same or better results in fewer hours. Protecting your personal time often leads to greater satisfaction in both your work and personal life, leading to greater productivity, and more creativity.

Plan for fun and relaxation. These are also an essential part of living a well-balanced life. Making time for yourself is important to staying happy and healthy. If you believe that the most important thing is to be happy in life then you can always make time to do something that will make you happy. Until you get into the habit of taking time for yourself, set aside time for you. Plan what you're going to do and make any necessary arrangements to ensure you'll be able to keep your commitment.

In life you make time for what you want to make time for. If something is important to you, don't push it aside dismissing it with "I don't have time for that right now." You are in charge of your own schedule—it's up to you to make time.

Joe Becwar, President of Joe Becwar Coaching & Consulting Group LLC, has embraced personal development, goal-setting, and the desire to improve his life since college while attaining his degree in social work. He has worked directly with some of the most successful names in business (Calvin Klein, Donna Karan) and their organizations, motivational teachers, and authors and speakers in the industry. Joe focuses on coaching executives, entrepreneurs, individuals in evaluating and achieving both personal and professional goals, assisting them to transform their lives and businesses. Visit *www. joebecwar.com* for more information.

GOALS OR NO GOALS? THAT IS THE QUESTION!

by Joseph (Joe) Becwar

You're right! To paraphrase Henry Ford, whether you think you need goals, or don't, you're right either way.

A. If you believe goals will help you, they will work.

B. If you believe goals won't help you, they won't work.

C. No one needs "stinkin' goals." But, if you use the right goals as a tool, you could get what you want, faster, easier, and with less difficulty.

What do you **really** want?

To lose weight, or have heads turn when you walk into a room? To have more time, or be able to enjoy the time you have with your family and friends? To have more money, or those things that financial freedom can bring? To worry less or have solutions to turn a dis-liked job into fun?

"In the absence of clearly defined goals, we become strangely loyal to performing daily trivia until ultimately we become enslaved by it."
Robert Heinlein

Today we will cover two tools that are easy and simple to use. First, the S.M.A.R.T. system. Second, a goal priority setting system.

Let's get started. A great, proven tool is using S.M.A.R.T. goals. The ones for smart people like you. What are they? Goals that are:

Specific

Measurable

Achievable

Realistic

Time-limited

Now, for an example, using one of the most popular "New Year's Resolutions,"—losing weight.

A "S.M.A.R.T." Plan for A New Appearance

"Map out your future, but do it in pencil." Jon Bon Jovi

Suppose you want "heads to turn," but realize losing some weight would really help. Being specific could be: "I will lose an ounce of weight every day for 30 days." It's also measurable, and you could write down: "I will weigh myself every Saturday morning, and measure my progress on a wall chart in the kitchen."

Now, is losing about two pounds a month achievable, for you? Is it realistic? Is it better than losing no weight, or gaining two pounds? Would two pounds a month of weight loss that adds up to about 24 pounds one year from now make a difference? Also called "baby steps," small accomplishments WILL get you there faster than no steps at all!

It did for me. I was able to lose 25 pounds in five months, through a combination of small changes in what I ate, and setting up an exercise plan of walking 5000 steps a day, five days a week, and joining a local fitness center that I used two or three times a week. Diet changes over the past three years had not helped me lose that weight. So it took a combination of changes to work. You may need more, or less.

Sure, it wasn't easy, and I didn't like going to a "gym", but it was close and I negotiated an excellent "deal." The trainer was nice, and it wasn't crowded. And one time, after I saw an elderly lady using her walker to get to the next "station," I was sort of "shamed" into continuing. I was paying for it, too.

It's time to mention flexibility. Things don't go according to plan, no matter how much we want them to. As Zig Ziglar tells the story, he was on a flight to Phoenix from Dallas, for a speaking engagement, the plane encountered a large thunderstorm. Did the pilot return to the airport in Dallas for another try? No, he altered course, and went around the storm, arriving at his destination a little later. Be sure you build in time for adjustments, whether it is for emergencies, financial challenges, or family situations. Goals are simply tools to help us. We don't want to become a "slave" to them, or allow you to "beat yourself up" over something small that can be dealt with reasonably.

Now, is losing two pounds a month realistic? Where are you starting from? What worked for you in the past? Why would you choose two instead of three, five, or ten? Does it make sense, or have you consulted your doctor to find out if a medical procedure is going to be needed? Will just walking for exercise be enough, or will a gym program, or a sports activity be useful? What diet changes will you make, small, or large? Cut carbs, double the servings of fruits and vegetables, eat smaller and highly nutritious meals, or all the aforementioned?

A coach's caution, "Always consult with your medical advisor before beginning any significant change in diet or exercise." Are there any medical conditions, medications, etc. that will affect what, how, and when you do things?

Time-limited, or specified, is essential. Will you do this short-term, for less than three months, or do you want to commit to a year or more? How often will you be monitoring your progress? Will you set weekly, monthly, and quarterly goals? How will you check this? Using a wall chart, keeping a journal, reporting to a friend or partner, or all of these?

S.M.A.R.T. Plan for A New Appearance – Summary

I will lose one ounce a day, 30 ounces a month, for 12 months, to achieve a new look for myself. I will check my weight every Saturday morning, and post it on a wall chart in my kitchen. I will be reducing my calorie intake by 600 per day, and will be walking a minimum of 5000 steps a day, five days a week, measured by a pedometer. I will keep a daily journal, recording my actions and progress, and keep my friend posted on this as my accountability partner. **Now, that wasn't too hard, was it? Does it make sense?**

As Denis Waitley said: *"The reason most people never reach their goals is that they don't define them, or ever seriously consider them as believable or achievable. Winners can tell you where they are going, what they plan to do along the way, and who will be sharing the adventure with them."*

Be aware of a few things. Is the goal to lose weight, or to look better by losing some weight? Is this a goal that you have chosen for yourself, or has someone else (spouse, partner, employer) told you to lose some weight? And a word of caution—avoid the "let down" after achieving your goal, by making it an ongoing process of improvement. As John Dewey said, **"Arriving at one point is the starting point to another."**

Are there other methods, or ways, to improve your appearance that you want to do along with weight loss, such as some muscle toning, improving your wardrobe, getting a different haircut, changing your attitude toward others and how you do things, smiling more, doing some affirmations, etc.? Maybe even reviewing your values, those you associate with, changing some habits, doing some volunteer work, reading some significant books, taking a course to improve your skills at home or work, or any number of new opportunities for the "new you."

"Vision without action is a daydream. Action without vision is a nightmare." Japanese Proverb

Goal Priorities

"Set priorities for your goals. A major part of successful living lies in the ability to put first things first. Indeed, the reason most major goals are not achieved is that we spend our time doing second things first." Robert J. McKain

Another tool I want to share with you is a brief exercise. Write down 10 goals you'd like to accomplish in the next year. Then, if you could accomplish one of these in the next 24 hours, which one would have the greatest effect on your life? Then circle it. "It" will usually jump out at you!

Choose another one. Would it be a health, family, financial, fun, or an educational goal? Then turn the page over, and set a time limit for it. Make a list of everything you could do to achieve it. Next "plug it into" the S.M.A.R.T. system. Then do something everyday to achieve it.

"To will is to select a goal, determine a course of action that will bring one to that goal, and then hold to that action till the goal is reached. The key is action." Michael Hanson

In conclusion, consider the following by Brian Tracy. If he was given only five minutes to speak, and could convey only one thought that would help you be more successful, he would say,

"Write down your goals, make plans to achieve them, and work on your plans every single day."

James Burow is a professional health coach in Edmonds, WA. He recently completed a one-year intensive Health Coach Training Program with Hilton Johnson Productions. He is a retired banker, former teacher (middle/high school and college), and has worked for the federal government, a private college, retail businesses, is a U.S. Navy veteran, and world traveler. He holds a B.A., M.S., and B.A.I.S. in business, and also coaches small businesses on marketing. *http://CoachJayBurow.com*

CONVERSATIONS WITH YOUR "KITCHEN TABLE COMPUTER GURU"

by Sherry Bowers

The weekend was finally here and I had invited a couple of my friends over for morning coffee. After we had updated each other on the office politics of the week and our latest family dramas, the conversation turned, as it frequently does when we get together, to brainstorming and the inevitable "how do I....?" computer and internet questions.

Sally started first."Hey, have you ever sold anything on eBay? A lady at Tommy's daycare said she was selling jewelry on eBay." Now Sally's mouth may have been asking me if I ever sold anything on eBay, BUT what she was REALLY asking me was how could "I" make money online.

You see in the 15 plus years of helping others discover and grow their internet and computer dreams, I have only REALLY been asked five questions. Questions that are critical also in today's economy! Everything else was just a variation of the Big 5.

1. How can I create an alternate income source?

2. How can I stay competitive?

3. How can I stay connected with others?

4. How can I improve my skills?

5. How can I learn this stuff when I am afraid?

So Sally wanted to be able to sell her handmade jewelry online too and create an alternate income stream. She had been juggling a part time office job with the needs of her family and it was causing everyone stress. I knew what she was really searching for was to be able to work a flexible schedule that would allow her to put her family first. Isn't that most of us want, but just don't know how to make happen?

So we talked about eBay and shopping carts, websites and promotion, consignment sites and drop shipping sites. I was able to help her prioritize her steps and provide her with the information, recommendations and assistance she needed to get started. Knowing that she had access to assistance for each step simply by calling her "Kitchen Table Computer Guru" gave her the confidence she needed. She was ready to go. We even set up a tentative date for her to give her notice at work which was very exciting.

All this talk had gotten Diane thinking. I could tell. She always chewed her lip when she was thinking about something serious. "You know," she said, "I was thinking about redoing my own website, with maybe a new design or something."

But I knew Diane was not really asking me about redoing her website. What she was REALLY asking me was "How can I stay competitive?" Diane is a realtor with her own Real Estate Broker's business. With the current economy, her traditional business had taken a huge hit. She needed to know how she could build upon her existing business and website and create something to add value to it and keep her competitive edge.

So we talked about her skills and what she loved about her real estate business. We talked about what lessons she was learning from the new economic conditions and what new problems this was creating for buyer and sellers as well as her agents. I suggested she might want to consider adding more of an educational or coaching focus to her website for buyers and sellers. Using that idea with a periodic newsletter would allow her to stay in front of potential clients longer than the competition. This led to more discussions about email lists, blogs and free housing seminars.

I could see the tension ease from her face and quickly be replaced with the ideas that started racing across it. She knew that she had her "Kitchen Table Computer Guru" available whenever she had a question. Together we had turned her problems into new solutions. I had helped her focus on her new goals and I made a note of the training tutorials I would send to her later that day.

Once all the business chatter had slowed down, it was Dorothy's turn. Dorothy had been a neighbor of mine for many years. She spoke up timidly. "My son called me yesterday and wants to get me a webcam for my computer, can you believe that? What on earth would I ever do with a webcam? They are for kids. Anyway, I wouldn't know the first thing about how to use one."

I nodded and smiled because I knew she wasn't REALLY asking what to do with a webcam. What she was REALLY asking me was "How can I stay more connected with my kids and grandkids."

I knew why her son wanted her to have one! I also knew how much she would enjoy it! With her son and grandchildren so far away, what a wonderful way to stay connected and still be able to watch them grow, to share the excitement of their first lost tooth and congratulate them on the award they received from school. So I explained how simple they were to hook up and use and all the different things she could do with it. She could see the kids whenever she wanted. She could record the grandchildren with it. She could print photos with it. I saw the excitement spread across her face. There was a twinkle in her eyes as they imagined the expressions and antics of her grandchildren and as she realized she could keep tabs on her only son, James.

Then came the "Yes, but's." "Yes, but I don't know how to hook it up or how to use it." Oh boy, Dorothy was going for 2 questions out of the Big 5 Questions! Can you guess what she was REALLY asking me? I bet you can. She was REALLY asking me "How can I learn how to do this when I am afraid?"

At this point we all laughed, because it was these four friends of mine that had dubbed me their "Kitchen Table Computer Guru." She knew I would be there to help her each step of the way. Of course I reminded her of that, which put her at ease. So we set a date for me to walk her through how to hook it up and go over some easy instructions on how to use it. By the time we were done talking, I thought for sure she was going to ask to borrow my phone so she could call her son and have him ship the webcam immediately.

Finally after listening to us girls carry on Tony joined in with a software issue he was having at work, "Did I tell you that I have the opportunity for a promotion at work? The only thing is, that it requires that I know how to create spreadsheets in Excel, and I only know how to use spreadsheets, not how to create them."

Well, you guessed it! He wasn't REALLY asking me about how to create spreadsheets. What he was REALLY asking me was "How do I improve my skills?" So I explained some of the basics about creating formulas, formatting Cells, Rows and Columns. I explained that there are many templates that can be customized to save time and effort. We discussed the types of spreadsheets that he would be making, so we could focus on the parts of Excel he really needed to learn. I made notes and promised I would create some custom training tutorials just for his specific needs. He was elated and I was more than happy to share what I knew.

By this time everyone was eager to get started on their new projects, so we said our goodbyes and everyone headed off to get started. I in turn, headed to my home office to email the information I had promised to Diane, Dorothy and Tony. It felt really good to know I was able to answer the questions they asked me as well as the REAL questions they didn't. Ah, the "Kitchen Table Computer Guru" struck again!

As you can see there are many reasons you may want to find Your Own "Kitchen Table Computer Guru." Someone who is easy to communicate with and either has the answers, or can direct you to those that do. It makes life easier, more productive and just plain more fun. The key is finding the perfect "Guru" for YOU.

So to help you in your hunt, here are several questions you should ask your potential guru, as well as some pointers to keep in mind.

1. Ask them to tell you a little about how they got into the computer and internet field. Listen to what they say as well as how they say it. Do they talk about their field with enthusiasm? Can you hear it in their voice? If they love what they are doing they will be more likely to go the extra mile to help you with your specific needs.

2. Ask them to describe the types of customers they work with. Who is their typical client? Does it sound like you? Do they work only with beginners, intermediate clients, advanced clients or clients at all skill levels? Do you feel that you could grow your abilities and still be able to work with them?

3. Ask them to tell you about their business background. Have they had their own business? Doing what? How long? This will tell you a bit about their life experiences and how broad their business knowledge is. The ability to combine technical expertise and business knowledge could be invaluable to you.

4. Ask them for testimonials or references that you could talk to. As with any business, there are good, legitimate ones and there are some not so good. By speaking with some former and some current clients you should be able to get a feel for what your "potential guru" is really like.

So if I have left you with some ideas, inspirations, or nuggets of information to help you on your technological adventure, I have done my job. Just remember, what is most important is getting your REAL questions answered, so keep hunting and asking until you do. You are worth it!

Sherry Bowers has been involved with the internet, website design and hosting for over 15 years. Her ability to translate technical issues into simple steps and communicate them to her clients in an easy to understand manner has been her key to success. Visit *http://www.showmehowcomputers.com/sq*

FLASH FORWARD

by Sherry Bowers

T he kitchen window was open. A cool breeze was blowing through as though trying to dry the hot tears that were streaming down Ruth's face and falling onto the front of her faded denim shirt. Washing breakfast dishes was taking an unusually long time at 1925 Maple Leave Avenue, Olive Bridge, Georgia.

Ruth labored with thoughts of what she could possibly do to turn this financial dilemma around quickly as it was already headed, in a downward spiral, at breakneck speed. Feeling hopeless, and weary of answering phone calls from sarcastic bill collectors; opening letters that threatened foreclosure, and trying to keep all these troublesome facts from her two children, was draining the life right out of this 5', 97 pound, hardworking, mother. She held an enormous capacity to find the good in just about anything life could hand her; but this time, she felt desolate and desperate. Ruth's marriage was in jeopardy and this was only amplifying the family's stress level.

She blew her nose, inhaled two, slow, deep breaths and trudged into her bedroom. She knelt, clasping her hands together, with elbows resting upon the yellow, chenille bedspread, and began verbally pouring her heart out. Trusting the higher power more than any mortal, she pleaded for help. The telephone was already unplugged and the drapes were drawn. All she wanted was to be left alone, so she could think.

Exactly one week to the day, at 5:00 a.m., Ruth's eyes opened wide. She bolted upright in her bed. Her mind was in total awe, as she began to recall the vivid dream she had just awakened from. She felt a sort of chill, as the hair on her body began to stand straight up! "My God, that's it," she exclaimed! Ruth ran out of the bedroom and headed toward the basement door totally forgetting her slippers! Descending the cold basement stairway, she looked around. She saw the wooden stepladder and the dented paint tray, next to the workbench. "Oh thank you, Spirit," she uttered, with a half cry, half shout, in her voice! "Thank you for loving me!" "Thank you for helping me!" "These are my tools," she said out loud!

As the children were eating their breakfast that morning, they noticed their mother seemed very happy about something. They questioned Ruth as to just what was making her eyes sparkle and her actions so quick. "Well children, I had the most wonderful dream last night, and I can hardly wait to tell you about it," she said. "It must have been an awfully good one," said Doug. "Yes, dear, it was." "Well, come on Mom, let's hear it," shouted Mindy! "Ok, strap on your seat belts, here goes. Hope you're both ready for this," she said, in a higher pitch than usual! "I had this dream last night, and it has given me the answer to my prayers," she told them. "I just have 'chicken skin' all over my body, every time I think about it," she exclaimed, while running her hand over her forearm, trying to calm herself!

"What is so exciting to me is that I know it will work," Mom said, excitedly! "Yes, keep going Mom," Mindy replied. "I dreamed that, all the elderly people, who have arthritis, and those who are widows, would rather have a woman paint in their home, than a man," she said. "I never considered this, but it is true, and I am going to do it," Mom stated with conviction. "Wow, Mom," the children said in unison, "go for it!" "You know, I have always been the painter around here anyway," Mom recalled. "Gee, that's right, Mom," Doug and Mindy, exclaimed! "You have a truck too," giggled Doug, as he teased her. The truth is that he thought it was pretty neat that he had the only Mother around who drove a truck! A red truck, no less!

After doing some checking around about what to charge Ruth placed an ad in the Want Ads section of the local newspaper the very next week. The ad needed to be brief. "Female Painter; neat; affordable, and available immediately," is how it read. The telephone rang constantly, the very next day. The calls came from women who wanted to have interior painting done. The quick response surprised the whole family.

The people who were calling, were telling Ruth, how they could not paint for themselves anymore due to their age and because they had arthritis? Would you believe it? Incredible as it may sound that is exactly who was calling her! Ruth knew only too well, that her "dream," was much more than a dream; it was not only an inspiration for her, but also an opportunity to change her life. She was grateful and willing, to give it her all. She was going to handle it like a lady on a mission!

Ruth made her dream a reality! In the process, she developed a thriving, successful business for herself. Step by step, month by month and year after year, she grew her dream business. It was hard work, but she was doing something that she had a real passion for. Ruth never grumbled about how hard it sometimes was. She was making new friends and being of valuable service to people at the same time. Helping others was always one of her priorities, and now she was sharing her talents with many people. She felt good about herself! She was her own boss, and loved what she was doing. What could be greater than that! She and her family began living an extraordinary life from then on.

After doing this for 15 years, Ruth discovered, to her dismay, that she could not continue the tight and strenuous work schedule any longer. The lifting and climbing up and down ladders, was beginning to take its toll on her body. How sad it made her, to have to concede to this reality. The years passed as she once again, worked for others, instead of for her self. It was not the same. She often would mention that she missed her former life, doing what she loved. "Painting was always the love of my life," she would say in a reminiscent tone of voice. "Maybe I should try painting on canvas next," she would say with a laugh.

Now, 40 plus years later, she founded a company called, Total Coach. Coming across this wonderful company has been another blessing for her. Through Total Coach, and the expert mentoring she receives, from Brian and Mike Litman, she finds that she can still perform the work she loves so much. This time, however, Ruth is doing it in quite a different manner. Now, she "coaches" others to do what she did. She shows them how to be their own bosses. She helps them find their passion in life and their inner voice as a call to action. Always encouraging, teaching and guiding, Ruth now helps people to discover what's truly meaningful to them, to develop their confidence, and to reach their goals for success, ever so patiently step by step.

"It is a win-win situation here at Total Coach," she says. "It is set up so everyone wins, and that is what makes it all so right," she says with pride.

Ruth Ota is semi-retired and lives in Hilo, Hawaii, with her husband. She is an author and has written two inspirational books, several dhildren's books and many helpful, insightful, and instructional books about the House Painting Profession.

Ruth enjoys teaching others create their own businesses; be their own boss; choose their own working hours; take the time off they need when the need is there; increase their self-esteem and self-confidence. To learn more go to:
http://www.helpfromunexpectedplaces.com/sq

BOOMERS WITH PURPOSE

by Patricia (Pat) Mora

"**B**een There... Done That... What's Next?"

As a Baby Boomer, Retired Corporate Officer, and Postmaster, I can honestly say: "Thanks for the ride... but I want off! You too? Our *"first 50"* years are about obligations and growth. The second half is the reward; the "me" time to enjoy life.

BUT... what if you aren't sure what you really want anymore? Ever feel like the "real you" got lost to career, family obligations, aging parents, and just surviving? Now is your "me" time, but... you ask: *"Who am I really?"*

Well, Boomers, Retirees, or those "ready to be" retired... THIS is the time to be reintroduced to an old friend. The REAL YOU! Then ignite the passion and purpose that remains waiting deep in your soul.

ASK YOURSELF THIS: *"So, WHO am I exactly?"*

Yes! Our first half is done! Obligations have eased. NOW is the time to simply be you! But, what does that *really* mean? *(Have you forgotten?)*

Looking at my past Government "in the box" education and experience of 31 years, an analytical pattern emerged. My positions of Systems Analyst, Certified Interviewer, Postal Auditor, and Postmaster Trainer just were part of the "big picture" utilizing my natural abilities, but not the deep desires of my heart.

Did I see this clearly while doing it? Of course not!

It took self-reflection, determination, much reading and analyzing plus mastermind friends to uncover (rediscover) the skills and talents I locked inside years ago.

How soon we forget our passions and talents from childhood!

Get In Touch With The Person You Are Now

When you do what you love, and love what you do! It puts excitement into waking up each morning! So if money were no object, what would you be doing all day right now?

Once we take the time to actually STOP and examine our God-given talents and identify what we are passionate about, the whole picture changes.

After retirement, I wanted to supplement my fixed income to include more "play time." I thought my successful career and 20+ years at my training and show horse ranch in Colorado surely was background enough for setting up the next step in life... Entrepreneurship.

Wrong!

Ever feel like an octopus looking everywhere at once, with tentacle arms waving wildly and grabbing all over the place? Yeah, me too! The mindset shift from structured corporate thriving to deep uncharted waters of the network-marketing abyss just didn't make sense!

Each of my tentacle arms were told to grasp a product to sell, a program to use, buy a tool over here, a tool over there, a training call five nights a week, a webinar three days a week, an arm waving "Buy more leads"... and on and on.

This confused octopus went nowhere! It was all tangled up in it's own flailing arms clutching 30 different things!

The only thing that grew was my frustration and credit card charges!

After FAILING at various MLM's (several times), I had enough! I decided this online entrepreneur stuff was not for me! Plus being **"TECHIE CHALLENGED"** didn't help either!

But... For some reason deep within, I was unable to just give up. It's not my style.

After three years of trial and painful, expensive error, I discovered how to incorporate my enjoyable skills from the past into what I felt called to do NOW. Bingo! One door opened after another.

Yes, my ever-patient husband and I have been ripped off by a professional scam artist, stolen from by Internet hotrods and beat up by high-pressure marketers and copycat cyber hype.

Just like the seasons of the earth, each of us has a "season" to progress through also. Some people get stuck in the cold season of winter all their lives. However, the sun remains shining. They are unable to see it.

I Still Believe!

I believe I have what it takes. I now understand I am a researcher and information messenger. I love to study, learn, and grow. I write and explain. MOST of all... I love to share! What about you?

Our powerful baby boomer generation has already experienced the results of survival and success. Now it's simply: *Boomers Unite!* This is an opportunity to "DO WHAT YOU WANTED TO DO ALL ALONG!"... and share with others.

If not now... WHEN?

Ask The Right Questions

Many of us know what we *"should"* do, but we have chosen. Not to because of all the emotional conflict and confusion of everyday life, simply because there are too many choices, too much Internet overload and sales ads screaming in our faces.

Many let careers define them. Some by how much money they make, the make of car, or the size of their house. Yes, these are fun rewards, but empty status symbols. It is the investment in *self* that counts in the long run.

My advice: Follow your heart. Your heart will not lead you wrong... but your mind might. Past limiting beliefs and stale, old programs on "auto rewind" will bring more of the same. True heart wisdom comes from within our core. This is where we connect to the power source.

Each step we take reveals a new horizon!

But first appreciate what you <u>do</u> know! The search is not outside of yourself. But within. Learning is NOT over just because you have retired. Now comes the enjoyable part!

It Is Not Too Late To Begin What You Can Become

Hey, don't be like my octopus with all her arms waving wildly, trying to grab everything someone says to do. You will tangle yourself up and go nowhere!

First: Define WHO you are.

Then: Discover WHAT you really want this time!

So many people are unable to answer these basic questions. Yet it is these same people who wonder why they keep getting more of what they don't want!

Question: What do you think about consistently? What is on your mind day in, and day out? Is this where your heart and dreams truly are?

<u>Remember:</u> Tune in to yourself first!

"Find your soul, and if it's still alive, poke it with a stick, find out which way it moves and then follow it." Ralph Waldo Emerson

---

Patricia Mora, the Boomer Advocate and Coach, is Founder and Publisher of Boomers With Purpose Unlimited, CoFounder of TEAM-BoomerPreneur Mastermind Group John Mora, Editor and Product Creation.

The vibrant Boomers With Purpose Recovery Network will help find your passion based, profit and fun filled purpose. Enjoy everyday living by recovering your deep passions and purpose. *www.BoomersWithPurpose.com, pat@boomerswithpurpose.com*

DON'T SELL OUT: ADD UP!

Get What You Want by Wanting More of What You Have

by Diane Chew

The average person has 60,000 thoughts a day and the vast majority are negative: "I'm too fat!" "We'll never get out of debt!" "I can't get it right!" No wonder it seems as if bad things keep happening—it's all we think about. Sell out to negativity, and it will take over your life.

Imagine the power of harnessing 60,000 POSITIVE thoughts each day. What we focus on GROWS. If we could learn to concentrate on the good things and add them up, we'd grow more.

Ok, I know. The concept of positive thinking has been around a long time. But how many of us are deliberately using it?

Most of us resist what's making us feel trapped or scared. And the more we resist our current "reality," the more it persists! So when it feels as if negativity has taken up a permanent home in your brain, don't give up. Switch to the positive, because the fastest way to get what you want is to want more of what you have.

"Oh no! Don't make me settle for what I have when what I have feels so awful!

I can hear your protest. I feel your pain! I was there myself, but I changed, and so can you. A simple three-step process will start you on the road to living a "success story" instead of a "stress story." And the good news, is that you can do it all in your head.

Yep—that's right. It's all about what you're thinking and how that's making you feel. The formula for wanting more of what you have so you can have what you want is:

Awareness – Acceptance – Action

AWARENESS - "What You Focus on Grows!"

Let's start with awareness of how you're thinking. If you're not satisfied with one or more areas of your life, it's tough not to think about it, right? The problem is that we live in an "attraction-based" universe. The law of attraction says, "like attracts like." The more we think negative thoughts, the more we attract others just like them.

Remember: we create what our day looks like by what we think about whether we realize it or not. Our thoughts lead to how we feel, and our feelings are powerful "attractors."

Conclusion: the more we think about what we <u>don't</u> want, the worse we feel about it, and the more we attract what we <u>don't</u> want.

I'll tell on myself as an example. My husband has a rare disability that affects his sensitivity to sound. He had to give up his career as a musician, and he can't tolerate noise of any kind. We're isolated in our home, can't go out to a restaurant or movie and it's hard to communicate unless I find the perfect pitch and tone.

Whenever he told me to be quiet (a frequent occurrence,) I'd feel sorry for myself (and him!) And that would take me off on a "negativity spree," thinking about ALL the things that were going wrong: losing my lucrative corporate job, a house needing serious maintenance, and the stress of trying to get my business off the ground. To say that negativity had taken up residence is an understatement.

Anything feel familiar? It's ok. The first step towards adding up the positives so that you want more of what you have is awareness of your thoughts and feelings. As we just notice the negative thoughts that are making us feel frustrated, trapped, or scared, we've taken a huge step towards attracting and manifesting what we really want.

ACCEPTANCE - "What You Resist, Persists!"

Now here's where so many of us fall flat on our proverbial faces. Once we're aware of the negative thoughts that are making us feel miserable and attracting more of what makes us feel miserable, we try to take action to change things.

I was well aware of what was making me feel depressed and trapped and I tried to take action by running away from my reality. I'd take any excuse to get out of the house or indulge in bad habits to avoid my negative thoughts and feelings.

One morning as I was pulling the covers over my head (again!) I realized I was in an endless loop of awareness, attempted action, awareness, and attempted action. I was living the "Insanity Loop of Resistance:" thinking, feeling and doing the same things and expecting different results.

But how could I drop my resistance? The light bulb went on when I questioned what I was truly resisting. It was how I felt about the situation. And the more I resisted my feelings—the more they persisted. The only way I could break the "Insanity Loop of Resistance" was to stop feeding my feelings and accept them.

This was a tough step. The idea of accepting my reality and my feelings about it, or heaven forbid, WANTING what I already had, felt akin to giving up. THAT WAS JUST NOT ACCEPTABLE! I was **not** willing to give up on what I wanted in life, but I **was** willing to accept my feelings about my current reality. It took some good crying jags, punching the bag at the gym, and furiously journaling to let it all out—but my resistance started to melt.

As I started to accept my feelings, I noticed that my flow of negative thoughts slowed down. And as they slowed down, my mind cleared up so I could take a different action, so I could FINALLY get a different result.

ACTION - "What's New vs. What's True?"

Now the third step in the formula: Awareness, Acceptance, and ACTION! But the action I'm suggesting is not what you might think. It's not about taking action to get OUT of your current situation. It's about looking for clues about everything that is going RIGHT with your life, so you can choose different thoughts about your reality.

"Impossible!" you say. "How can I choose a different thought when what I'm focusing on is TRUE?? Well—it may be true, but more importantly: "what's new?" I realized I had to come up with a new way to think about my situation to get the law of attraction to work **for** me, rather than **against** me. I had to add up the positives and want more of what I had, to attract more of what I wanted.

I went on a rampage of appreciation, listing what was going right with my life: big and small. Instead of feeling frustrated about what I couldn't do with my husband, I focused on how much we liked to laugh together (quietly!) Instead of thinking about our dwindling accounts, I listed all my accomplishments and the skills I could use to help my clients. Instead of dwelling on all the needed maintenance, I enjoyed my thriving plants.

Believe me. It took practice and persistence. The more I was able to add up positive thoughts, the better I felt, and the more I began to want what I already had. As I started to want what I had, other things started to change. We cleared out clutter to create the space for renovations to our home. Opportunities for joint ventures with colleagues materialized. My husband and I discovered activities that we COULD do together: from collaborating on his new endeavors with photography to dancing at home to the soft strains of an acoustic guitar.

The trick with the action step is to choose a different thought that moves you even incrementally up the emotional scale, since when you're in despair, it's nigh on to impossible to find a positive thought that will take you on a quantum leap to joy.

Try taking baby steps. I looked for ANY thought that made me feel slightly more positive. Often I had to choose a thought that had absolutely NOTHING to do with the issue making me feel lousy in the first place. But remember—it's not about what's true—but what's new? "Inch by inch, everything is a cinch," and that's true of adding up the positives. Don't sell out to negativity. Find what's working. Feel better. That's how you move towards wanting more of what you have so you can have what you want.

Diane Chew is a professional success coach in New Hope, PA, working with teams and individuals to help overcome the conscious and subconscious blocks to their success. She blends her scientific, spiritual and corporate backgrounds to address the unique needs of each client. Diane graduated from CoachU and Corporate Coach University, is an advanced certified EFT practitioner and has coached for over 20 years inside and out of the corporate environment. For email coaching tips, visit: *http://www.dianechew.com/sq*

SECRETS TO AN EXTRAORDINARY LIFE

by Doug Evans

S ecrets of an extraordinary life! WOW! Isn't this something we all wish would suddenly be unveiled to us? Maybe a flashing neon sign in the sky one day that says Doug, Mary Ann, whatever your name is—*THIS* is your secret!

We'll it doesn't work that way. I think there is just one secret and that is—be happy. The big question is how do I do that? How? We'll talk about some key steps. Steps most people never bother with, that will darn near always get you to happiness if that is what you truly want.

Happiness is so universal that Harvard University, one of the most prestigious schools in the county, offers a course one it. Over 20 % of the students take this course. It is not a blow off course but a class where some of the best young minds in the country realize that this very well could be THE secret to an extraordinary life.

I have been a student of personal development, leadership, motivation and self improvement for years. I have read more books than a dozen people combined. I have attended seminars, spent thousands of dollars, enrolled in many, many classes and listened to more CD's than anyone, other than my wife, could imagine. I have worked closely with icons in this field. I have worked with Vic Johnson, Bob Proctor, Mike Litman, and Frank Gasiorowski. I then reflected on all this knowledge and conclude there are 10½ key steps that should and will make you happy. These steps WILL let you live the extraordinary life.

Remember an extraordinary life is different for everyone. For some it could be money, for others it is love, family, recognition and on and on. Whatever is right for you is what you need to pursue. My 10 ½ steps will work for everyone. What are they? We can't cover them all today or in the detail my all day classes do. Nevertheless, here are 7 of the important steps.

Step 1 - DREAM. Most people don't take the time to dream any more. Many have forgotten how. Your life starts with dreams. It helps you know what you want, and what is important to you. Everyone one of us wants something. Probably you desire many things in order for you to live your dream life. What are those "things"? Have you spent the time to really, really think about what it is that you truly want? Or, are you so darn busy that day after day just passes you by? Do you settle for less than you really want? Way too many of us do.

So... set aside some quiet time. You need some uninterrupted time, where you can kick back and just dream. Dream as you did when you were a kid. No fears, no limitations, no worries about how will you realize these important dreams. Take those dreams no matter how farfetched you initially think they are and write them down. Cherish those dreams, guard them, and protect them!

"Taking the risk to follow your heart gives energy to our future and breathes life into our dreams." Debbie Ford

Step 2 - SET GOALS. You have established your dreams, now it's time to develop a plan to help you reach those dreams. It's now the "how" part of the planning. Goals need to be SMART goals. Smart goals are specific, measurable, attainable, realistic, and include a specific time frame for each step.

Goal setting is your everyday map on how to find the hidden treasure- your dreams and your happiness. Goals are about what you are going to accomplish. They are about action. They are specific action steps you will take to chase your dreams. Goals require a commitment. You have to really, really want to accomplish your dream. If you are not 100% committed, they will never happen. Goals are magic and you have to treat them like magic.

Be sure to set goals for a balanced life. Balance is the key to keeping you focused and almost always is the key to overall happiness. Be sure to set financial, spiritual, personal, family, and health goals.

Chasing goals is hard work. You need to be accountable. You need a kick in the pants or a pat on the back all the time. Goals are often better achieved by not doing them all yourself. You have to be real tough. You have to be as tough as the nastiest Marine Core Drill Sergeant you can find. Consider enrolling in one of the goal programs that are out there (contact me for a couple great ones) or hire a coach to push you in the process. A coach can also make sure you aren't pursuing too few or too many goals.

Remember goals are all about planning and the next step-action.

"All who have accomplished great things have had a great aim, have fixed their gaze on a goal which was high, one which seemed impossible." Orison Sweet Marden

Step 3 - ACTION. All the dreaming in the world, all the goal setting, all the planning can be picture perfect but without action, nothing will happen. Nothing will be achieved. You need to get out there and take those steps you decided that you needed to do, and when you need to do them. Action is where so many fail. Ensuring action, being accountable is why many people need and opt for a coach. If you are a hockey nut like me, the best game plan, the best players in the world, perfect ice does nothing to help you win, or score a goal, until you drop the puck and get going by taking action. Don't stand around and be a fan or a spectator of your life. Get going! Take little steps. Start now. As you get going you will build momentum. Momentum is what builds success.

"You don't have to get it right, you just have to get it going!" Mike Litman

Step 4 - KEEP BALANCE IN YOUR LIFE. Most people who are not happy, who have crisis after crisis in their life focus on one aspect of their dreams and become obsessed with this aspect for a long period of time. When we have dreams and goals in our lives that are professional, financial, personal, family etc., we can't stay imbalanced in anyone area for too long. Focus is a mandatory part of success but imbalance takes it over the edge. We all become imbalanced for a short period of time. A deadline on a big project means we'll probably work some long hours for a few days—not weeks or months. If we decide to take time off and kick back on the water, if we do it too long, we lose our jobs or businesses. Constantly look back and be sure that you are taking time for all areas of your life. Make time; block out time. Whatever you need to do, do it. This is one area I fight with folks about all the time. I can't tell you the number of divorces I have seen, the troubled son or daughter I have heard about that is 99% due to Mom or Dad never ever taking their focus off work. Today with e-mail, pagers, cell phones etc., we can always be connected. Employers often require us to be connected. Don't get crazy. Don't go overboard. It's your life, your dreams. Don't let anyone, anyone steal them!!

"Just as your car runs more smoothly and requires less energy to go faster and farther when the wheels are in perfect alignment, you perform better when your thoughts, feelings, emotions, goals, and values are in balance" Brian Tracy

Step 5 - SHARPEN THE SAW. Keep learning. Keep growing. Keep educating yourself everyday Ask yourself each day-what did I learn? Don't stand still. Read, and then read some more, attend classes, listen to CD's in your car, watch DVD's but keep learning—never ever stop learning!!

"The learning and knowledge that we have, is, at the most, but little compared with that of which we are ignorant." Plato

Step 6 - HAVE GRATITUDE. We are all so blessed and many of us take it for granted. Take time each day and realize deep down all that you have—not only what you don't have. Take time to reflect each day to realize how truly blessed you are. If you are spiritual, thank your creator. I try to thank God every day. I also suggest keeping a gratitude journal and fill it out just before you go to sleep. You'll be shocked on how much better you sleep!! Start a gratitude habit today!

When Pope John Paul II was asked what heaven was, he said – "gratitude."

Step 7 - FF BAMA. This is not a busty gal from down South! It is an abbreviation you need to remember. It wraps everything together. It's the key to an extraordinary life all in one big enchilada. You really need to follow this with enthusiasm. It can be summarized by the quote, by the following secret:.

"Face and Conquer your fears, have Faith, Believe in Yourself, have the Attitude of Greatness at all times, Capitalize daily on Momentum, and Take Massive Action each and every day!" Doug Evans

---

Doug Evans is a success and abundance coach, speaker, motivational teacher and author based in the Metro Detroit area. Doug helps people uncover and strengthen the power they already have to live the life of their dreams. He has developed a special 10½ point system that enables individuals to advance from stuck and frustrated, to powerful and soaring. He also hosts the popular weekly Missing Power blog talk radio program.

Doug is a CPA whose firm helps small and medium size business owners increase their profits and grow their businesses. Contact him at:
doug@discoveryourmissingpower.com

WHAT DOES IT TAKE TO LIVE AN EXTRAORDINARY LIFE

by Doug Evans

D ifferent people have different ideas about what an extraordinary life is like according to our beliefs and values. To some it may be about having lots of money, to others it may be about traveling, fame, or acquiring material things. To me is about acknowledging and appreciating life, and all it has to offer.

I will attempt to describe what, in my opinion, it takes to have an extraordinary life. In no particular order:

LAUGHTER: How often do you laugh? I mean really laugh. We don't laugh often enough. Most people take life way too seriously to take time out for a good laugh. Laughter goes beyond feeling good at the moment. In her book *A Better Brain At Any Age: The Holistic Way To Improve Your Memory, Reduce Stress And Sharpen Your Memory*, Sondra Kornblatt describe the many health benefits of laughter and how it can really help you feel better for a long time. Laughter helps the pituitary gland release pain suppressing opiates.

Laughter can also lower blood pressure, increase blood flow and thus improve oxygenation of the blood, workout the diaphragm, facial, back and leg muscles, reduce stress, increase the response of disease and tumor killing cells, defend against respiratory infections, increase memory and learning, and improves alertness, focus and creativity.

Laughter has other benefits as well. It puts us in the now, and it is only in the now that we can experience happiness. Laughter makes a situation less serious and more tolerable, so you don't worry as much. Laughter diffuses three of the most painful feelings; fear, anger and boredom. It lifts us up and makes life worth living.

A playful approach to every day life occurrences makes us healthier and happier.

I WILL DO NO HARM: Many people will go through life acting and reacting to events without thinking that their actions and their words have consequences. They live in a bubble and only think of themselves and what they want, what they want to accomplish, not considering other people's thoughts and emotions. I am not saying that we have to think about everyone else's opinions, thoughts or emotions before making a decision. If that was the case, then we would end up pleasing everyone else except ourselves, and we must be true to ourselves above all. What I am trying to explain is that whatever we want to accomplish in our lives, we must do so because it's not only for our best benefit but the greatest good of everyone. Our intentions and actions must lead everyone to a win-win outcome.

POSITIVE MENTAL ATTITUDE: This is CRITICAL to live an extraordinary life. Without a positive mental attitude we are doomed to permanently fail at whatever we aspire to accomplish before even trying. Failure does not exist until you decide to quit, until you give up and decide to accept it as permanent. We must understand that temporary defeat only makes us stronger and wiser, preparing us for the eventual success. If you try an approach and that doesn't work, try something else.

Think outside the box. Don't ask yourself why or why me? These are the most useless questions in the universe, blocking the mind from possible solutions. Instead, ask yourself "What is another way to approach this situation?" This question forces your mind to open up to different perspectives, and more potential solutions for the situation. Imagine if Edison would have quit after failing thousands of times in his attempt to develop the electric light bulb. Instead, he viewed each failure as the elimination of a solution that didn't work, thus moving him a step closer to one that did work. He knew that anything worthwhile takes persistence. Learn the *process* of life, not just the outcome.

TAKE CARE OF YOURSELF: People have probably heard this a million times. Then, how come most people don't take the time to do what they need to do to be at their best of health? Eat a healthy, balanced diet, get plenty of rest, exercise consistently, drink plenty of water, quit smoking if you smoke, drink in moderation. This is not rocket science. This is the age of information. Information is so easy to access, there is no excuse to say, "I didn't know what to do, or how to do it." Your body is your soul's temple. It needs you to make the right decisions and you need it so that you can live a long and healthy life.

Another aspect of taking care of your self is taking time to nourish your spirit. Whatever you choose or need to do to recharge your batteries. For some it may be exercising (this one is a double whammy as it is as good for your mind as it is for your body), meditating, practicing yoga, reading, taking a bubble bath or whatever. Taking 20–30 minutes a day to just be you is not much to ask. After all, the rest of the people in your life use the other 30 hours or so. Take off all of the other hats you wear and just take time to be the original you. You cannot give what you don't have within yourself.

GRATITUDE: We have the tendency to go through our busy lives just going from one thing we have to do to another. A "to do list" if you will, that we feel has to be completed every moment. We feel that we have to do as much as we can in as little time as possible to feel productive. What burden we put on ourselves! We put such demands on our bodies and spirit that they (body and spirit) complain by feeling overwhelmed, stressed out, depressed, chronically tired and/or ill.

Listen to your body and your spirit. If you feel like any of the above I just described, take Time Out. Take a few minutes daily to look deep within yourself at what's really important to you. This is probably closer to you than you think. We pay so much attention to what we want and don't have that we don't even see what we already have. We take it for granted. Make it a daily practice to look and find things to be grateful for. The more basic it is, the more likely it's taken for granted.

Take for example, the daily functions of our body such as breathing, walking, swallowing, our brain function, and our senses. Every cell of our body that knows exactly what it's supposed to do, when to do it, how to do it and we don't even have to intervene. It's our ability to communicate within. The list goes on and on. None of these are conscious, and we do take them for granted, yet it is devastating when we lose even one of these functions. Just ask anyone that has suffered a stroke or some kind of neurological injury and has not lost the ability to talk! With just this one aspect of our being, our list of things to be grateful for is quite long. What about the roof over our heads and the food on our table? The list is literally endless.

This attitude of gratitude is particularly important if you feel that you are in a low point of your life due to illness, financial difficulties, difficulties in your relationships, and feel stressed or depressed. Begin and end your day with gratitude, even for the things that you may "perceive" as bad. There is always a lesson to learn with each difficulty. Look for it, embrace it, and move forward. This goes hand in hand with what I described earlier about a mental positive attitude. When you have an attitude of gratitude, by default, you also have the latter.

FORGIVENESS: This may be the single most difficult thing to practice. Particularly, forgiving ourselves. As human beings, we are bound to be harmed or offended by someone else's actions and/or words. We may find ourselves having negative feelings such as jealousy, anger, or resentment to deal with. These feelings are only affecting you, not the person on the "receiving" end. The only way to find peace within ourselves is to practice forgiveness. And, forgiveness takes practice. To forgive is not easy, but we can do it. We can rise above into new ways of thinking and feeling if we just give ourselves permission to do so.

Diana Samalot lives in Port Saint Lucie, Florida with the love of her life Jim, her two teenage twin daughters, Giselle and Gabriella, their three dogs, Faith, Major and Roxie and their cat Shadow. Her life experiences, dedication, understanding, desire to help people and patience makes her a compassionate coach for people who want embark in a journey of self discovery, self empowerment and growth. Diana helps people discover who they really are, their gifts and strengths that are within them but undiscovered and undeveloped to make possible the positive changes in their lives that they need not just to survive but to thrive and to overcome self limiting beliefs for those that have the strong desire to do so. For more about Diana go to *http://www.doitnowcoach.com/sq*

THE UNCOMFORTABLE COMFORT ZONE

by Norma Costello

" **C** hange will never take place until the pain to stay the same is worse than the pain to change." John Maxwell

How comfortable is your comfort zone? It's amazing how VERY uncomfortable people can be in their lives, but are not willing to make changes. Do you feel that your status quo or comfort level is more or less like sleeping on a bed of nails? Is it contracted, tight and protected simply out of fear to change? How much or how little personal satisfaction do you have in your career, relationships, personal health, and/or spiritual life? Do you procrastinate, bombard and sabotage yourself with negative thoughts, look for exterior 'solutions' to the interior turmoil in your life? (Such as drugs, alcohol, sex, workaholism, etc.)

If you stub your toe, you will immediately have a reflexive action to grab it, rub it, and check it out. Maybe you will put a band aid on that throbbing toe and wear comfortable shoes for a while. When you have a nagging feeling that something has to change in your life, what do you do about it? How long do you wait and let this 'something' grow into a much bigger issue? For example, some people stay in abusive relationships that would be for others like sleeping on a bed of nails. These abusive relationships may have been precipitated with a series of poor choices, denial, and a feeling of low self worth, hopelessness, etc. But, the choice to remain confined lies within the person's ability to move out of this perception of comfort. Then, finally! The pain to remain in that 'uncomfortable comfort zone' is more than the pain to make the change. Tired of sleeping with the enemy? (**Whatever** that might mean to you) Then, why not try a comfortable mattress, for a change? Do you know how to define your problem? It's more than a stubbed toe, so why not reflexively do something about it?

I was married to a dentist for over 30 years. When his patients had a toothache, there wasn't a lot they were able to do productively until they took care of the pain. They would call in the middle of the night, Christmas Day, and sometimes even show up at our front door! But, they were in obvious pain. It might have started out as a little twinge of discomfort, but left unchecked became an abscess. As a result of waiting in discomfort until the dental issue grew, a little 'drilling and filling' was necessary, or possibly even the dreaded root canal to eradicate the decay and get the patient back to oral health. Why not use the discomfort of your life and make positive changes before you get caught up in the tidal waves or root canals of life? This should hold true when you experience mental or emotional pain as well as physical pain. What is the source of your discomfort? Have you let it go unchecked hoping that it will magically correct itself? Is it time for the dentist to get to the 'root' of your problems?

"If we're growing we're always going to be out of our comfort zone."
John Maxwell

Balancing your life—body, mind, and spirit—is a way to keep the flow of your life 'on purpose.' It is a conscious choice. Determine what is not feeling comfortable in your life, and welcome the changes that bring you new beginnings. If you are feeling fear that is keeping you from trying new things, finding a better job, taking the first step of an exercise class, working on a relationship (or getting out of one), or even skydiving, you must move past the fear. It's perfectly natural to experience some fear when you are moving past your comfort zones and 'out of the box.' It is a process, and can be achieved with baby steps. Of course, you can try to stay where you are. And that's a choice, too. But change is constant, and inevitable and the rest of the world is going to change with or without your conscious involvement in the process. The funny thing about making your uncomfortable comfort zone a little bit more comfortable is that once you step outside of the status quo, and push yourself a little more towards the vision you have for your life, it gets to be a healthy and exciting habit! You see the big picture more clearly. You don't have a vision? Find yours and energetically and passionately reach towards it. It's only a thought and a dream turned into an action away. Unleash your potential to dream big dreams!

"Cherish your visions and your dreams as they are the children of your soul; the blue prints of your ultimate accomplishments."
Napoleon Hill

Success in life is directly related to the amount of courage and faith you have to dream big and to believe that all things are possible. To discover and embrace the innate wisdom that lies within the core of your soul, and to put that wisdom into action, is to achieve your dreams. You must clearly define and crystallize your dreams and your vision of life by putting your positive thoughts, energy, faith and action into the steps necessary for their fulfillment. W. Clement Stone believed that whatever the mind of man can conceive and believe, it can achieve. Napoleon Hill spoke about the God-given ability of each person to achieve his or her goals based on the belief that this is a destiny or 'calling' of the soul's fulfillment. It is the ability to trust the infinite possibilities of life, moving past the fear of failure, and forward towards the energy of success. To be able to see the big picture, and see yourself in that picture with a smile on your face. This requires an awareness of your self limiting comfort zones. This requires the ability to persist with determination, letting go of old habits and beliefs that do not serve you and block the vision of your life's purpose. *Nike* really understood this concept with their logo, 'Just Do It'. So, be grateful for your dreams, and be joyful that you have chosen to take action to make your dreams come true!

Some Practical Steps to "<u>Create</u>" Positive Changes in Your Life And Stepping Out of Your Comfort Zone

1. Analyze your comfort zone. Determine if you have an imbalance in your body, mind or spirit. What is missing from your life? What is causing discomfort—or blocking your growth?

2. Be specific about areas that you have determined to change, or work on, and write down the specifics… i.e. weight loss, career change, improved relationships. (Honesty is the best policy here.)

3. Find a trusted accountability partner, life coach, or supportive group of friends to share your concerns and stumbling blocks with. Reaching out to others who are working on the same goals or issues is a great way to move forward.

4. Focus on your gifts, talents, and passions, in establishing a clear vision and goals for your life. What are you passionate about?

5. Remember that a **positive attitude** is the catalyst for transformation and progress.

6. Be grateful for the ability to breathe…*aaaahhhhh*. Ground yourself in the present moment, and don't focus on what you perceive as past failures. Look at past experiences as simply

stepping stones to your ultimate goals, leading you to expansion.

7. Keep your self talk positive!! Move towards what you WANT, and don't give power to what you DON'T WANT... "I want to be healthy." (Not, "I don't want to be fat.")

8. Don't take life too seriously—laugh often and get others to 'laugh their heads off' with you.

9. Remember that you are a work in progress, and if you don't like something, change it!

Norma Costello is a mother and grandmother, lover of people, an author, motivational speaker and life coach, specializing in guiding people back to the shore of higher thought and more productive living. She believes in balancing body, mind and spirit, and finding the passion and gifts within each individual. She helps each person she encounters to see life with a new perspective, much as an adventure. Norma is knowledgeable about loss and grief, forgiveness, and new beginnings. She believes in the empowerment of the individual and the transformation, co-creation and reinvention of self. To find out more visit *www.backtoshore.com*

TRUE PARTNERSHIPS

by Stephanie McMillan

L ook around you. How healthy are the relationships you see? Are your friends, family, associates engaged in meaningful, fulfilling, loving, empowering relationships? Are both parties inspired to follow their dreams and aspirations? Can they say and do what they please without repercussion? More likely than not what you're seeing are individuals going through the motions of a meaningful relationship, but for a variety of reasons are probably hiding their true selves.

What would it be like if we had "True Partnerships"? True partnerships are relationships where love, peace and power reside equally. No one person in these relationships bullies, berates or ignores the other. Imagine a world where *all* relationships were true partnerships. Sound impossible?

Forming true partnerships doesn't mean we have to start over with new relationships. It can start with the ones you are currently in. Remember relationships aren't limited to spouses. True partnerships can be developed with our parents, our children, our close friends, our coworkers etc. All of those relationships have a positive or negative affect on your life, and the lives of those around you. Wouldn't it be better if they were all positive? Let's explore how we can accomplish this.

Having true partnerships requires baring our souls. It can be scary exposing our true selves and vulnerabilities. Most of us at one time or another has done just that. What happened? Did the people closest to you shake their heads in disbelief? Did they discount your ideas, abilities and desires? Sometimes it only takes once for us to get shot down and we never expose our selves again. We can go through our entire lives pretending to be someone else. How sad.

A few of us do have close friends who will support us through whatever we decide to venture into. They want us to succeed and be happy. Let's take a look at our spouses and significant others. How supportive are they when you decide to show a side of your personality they have never seen before? Do they say you're acting very peculiar? Do they shout you down, telling you your ideas will never work or are stupid? Do they tell you that you embarrass them? Or do they just flat out ignore you?

It could be that they go all out to help you do what makes you happy. There are a few relationships out there where individuals are getting the support they need, but more likely than not, you're probably not in one of those. What I am suggesting here is going to take some soul searching. I mean you need to know what it is you really want. For some of you, your desires have been buried for so long it may take several weeks or even months for you to compile a list of what those needs actually are.

Sometimes we are in bad relationships. During your evaluation process be mindful that some relationships are not candidates for true partnerships. Let those relationships go. Allow those individuals to find someone who better mirrors their unique and special personality traits. Don't hang on to relationships that you know in your heart can never be true partnerships.

Distinguishing the relationships that you feel are valuable, and turning them into true partnerships, is what we want to develop. Initially you will want to let the individuals, with whom you want a true partnership with, know what your goals are concerning to the relationship. If your initial evaluations are correct, more than likely you are going to get a positive response once you initiate the change.

Most people want happy healthy relationships. They want to be supported, empowered, respected and loved. It's all about love. Your next step is that scary part; exposing who you really are and what your real needs are, the ones that you have been hiding for so long. This interaction requires a level of commitment on both parties to support one another regardless of what they hear the other person say. Your brain is going to remind you of past experiences where you exposed your true self and experienced pain. Don't listen. You have to work through the fear to get to the good stuff!

Life was not meant to be spent hiding who you really are! During your initial sharing session you may want to keep notes and/or bring notes to the session so you don't forget anything you want to share. It can be an emotional experience. Remember, you are only sharing what your needs are. Your partner will have their turn to share their needs.

This is also a time to forget the past. As human beings our nature is always reverting to the past. We don't know what the future will hold but we have to live in the now. The past is over, today is a brand new day, and you are going to be doing things differently from now on. You will want to continue this sharing process. This isn't a onetime thing. It's going to take time and commitment over the long term. Keep sharing, supporting and loving those partners as the equals they are. The more you share and support, the stronger the relationship becomes. Remember most of what I have shared here was directed at spouses and significant others. It needs to apply to all of your relationships, both personal and professional. Remember to be patient with one another. The rewards are boundless.

Studies show that the happiest people around the globe are happy because of the relationships they have. Relationships keep us healthy, not only emotionally but physically and mentally. Your willingness to embark on a lifelong change will have far reaching benefits, not only in your world but in the world of all you interact with. Your ability to develop true partnerships means no one is "in charge" of the other. No one individual has the right to bully, belittle or berate another trying to get them to be more like them.

We need to honor our uniqueness. Ignore what the media tells is the right or wrong way to be. We are all equals. That may seem scary to some of you, and totally ridiculous to others. We all have unique talents, abilities and characters. We are all *special*. Please be alert. We are bombarded daily with negative thoughts and ideas by the TV, radio and newspaper. Our culture tries to divide us based on color, national origin, male or female, and wealthy or poor. You are cultivating this magnificent being, known as you. As you go through your daily travels be an observer. Make a positive difference in other people's lives. Imagine what our world would be like if we *all* treated one another as equals!

I am asking you today to take a step back. Take the risk. Be a third party observer of your own life. Look at your relationships. Do you see some imbalances or some unhealthy interactions? Take the steps you need to rectify them. Determine what you truly want and need. Openly express your true wants and needs to your friends and family. Make sure you are clear that you want them to express their wants and needs to you as well. Let them know that they are special to you.

Make a pact that going forward, no one person has more value or power than the other. Your life will never be the same. Not only will these partnerships have a dramatic and positive impact on your life, you will also be affecting the consciousness of the entire planet. Let's do it together, one relationship at a time.

Stephanie McMillan's lifelong passion has always been to help people live more fulfilling lives. She has done this through various venues. As a health coach, her focus is co-crafting a wellness plant to meet your unique needs. She frequently speaks on the topic of wellness. Her most recent speech; "Health; it's not about insurance" targeted the differences between allopathic medicine and naturopathic medicine. Stephanie's "40-Day Life Dare" is a total, life changing wellness plan. Stephanie's broad knowledge base incorporates both eastern and western healing modalities. You may reach her at *www.StephanieMcMillan.com*

"SHOOT FOR FOREVER"

by Stephen (Steve) Jennings

Ageless Keys to Living Your Longest, Strongest and Most Fulfilling Life

In this relatively short passage, I intend to share with you a few "Ageless Keys" to living your Strongest, Longest and most fulfilling life. With these KEYS, you can look, feel and perform like you were decades younger, and gain your greatest chance of controlling the sands of time.

Most Important Key

However, you must first fully grasp the absolute most important "key", the one that YOU provide, or none of the other keys will provide their greatest benefit.

Very little will happen until you first dream and believe you can be more youthful and live your longest. **You bring about what you believe about.** I would suggest you even state your belief out loud, as your body believes every word you say.

"Thinking young" is fine, but you must believe you can achieve it—that you can extend your greatest biological potential—and it must matter to you greatly, down to the deepest strands of your DNA. With this mindset, all else good will follow. You must also be ready for the "keys", have a mighty reason and desire to apply them, possess the daily motivation and find your PURPOSE for living a lifestyle that will reap you the richest of rewards.

People have to be ready and desire to change and improve, to believe, have faith, and work, and do them all consistently. That's when the magic happens. Then the transformation of your body, your health and your best life can happen in the most wondrous of ways.

NOTE: Before you move on, I want to STRONGLY re-emphasize these incredibly important points of BELIEF and PURPOSE. Please do not race onward without keeping this fundamental understanding in your mind. If needed, re-read the beginning few paragraphs again, and ALLOW them permeate your mind, body, and soul.

An Illusion, A Lie

Being closely connected with the fields of health, nutrition science, fitness and human performance for nearly 40 years, personally and professionally, I've witnessed more than most with regard to the pursuit of anti aging and longevity.

So, first off, let me state that there's an unacceptable, BS premise that must be eliminated. Many doctors will tell you that aging, and the usual pain and expense that go along with it, is just an inevitable part of getting old.

Let me tell you something: That's an illusion. In fact, it's a downright lie.

Don't buy into the obsolete mindset that you're just going to get old and decrepit and suffer from age related diseases like everybody else. Don't think for a second that your body's declining health and appearance and signs of aging are a normal part of aging and that your hands are tied to do anything about it. Far from it!

The so-called "normal aging" most people experience isn't so normal at all! But, by the way you choose to live and what you actually believe, you'll either increase or diminish your health, appearance and best chance for longevity.

BS Assumptions

You don't have to give in to the feebleness, disease, and memory issues associated with aging – or at least the way most people experience aging. These symptoms are absolutely not "inevitable." We've been fed a boatload of BS assumptions, myths and insults to human intelligence forever.

Yes, aging is a natural occurrence, however so many of the things we think are "natural" such as tiredness, aches and pains, weakness, inflexibility and most age related degenerative diseases are not natural at all!

Now, these signs of aging can certainly happen if you proceed with your life like most folks do. However, by employing the "keys", you won't have to just sit back and "get old" like everybody else—you can experience a lifetime of youth that few ever do.

In Your Hands

In the world, we lose about 100,000 people to "aging" every day. We lose their talents, their relationships, and their ability to solve problems. All these folks could be helping the world become a better place, but they're gone.

My friend, your health and your best chance for longevity is in your hands.

Please listen carefully: You have a choice regarding the aging process.

With today's indisputable science, we now know that how much and how fast your body's internal clock ticks away doesn't depend greatly on genetics (perhaps 30%), but **from the choices you make**. You can choose to be "too busy", "not have the time" or find a million other lame excuses rather than care for yourself. Make an effort, not an excuse.

You see, most times you pave your own road to longevity.

Repeat Offender

Most of the conditions and damage that we falsely attribute to "aging" are self-inflicted through lack of proper movement, unhealthy "foods", unhealthy habits, and our less than healthy mindsets.

You can choose to feed your body low grade garbage that'll never supply it the quality nutrition it requires, have negative thoughts, get very little exercise, body movement or circulation, or you can choose to invigorate it to be its magnificent best by following the special "keys." If however, you continue with poor choices, then you become a repeat offender, and the consequences of aging become much worse. When the hammer comes down, don't say you didn't see it coming.

Health Held Hostage

Our health is held hostage mostly by our own doing. However, when you choose to treat the body respectfully, get it in balance by employing the special "keys", it has a marvelous, almost miraculous ability—an internal logic—to self-correct virtually all of the health challenges it may be facing as well as move towards its ideal weight.

What do you believe? What are you thinking? When you choose to change and improve your thoughts, you will change your world.

You can age rapidly, fall apart and breakdown like most everyone else , or you can age much more slowly, and not just "age gracefully," but "age greatly!" You can sustain a high level of wellness seen through top physical and mental stamina, smooth working, pain free joints, flexibility, a strong immune system, great digestive health, energy when you need it, sharp reflexes, a sharp mind and lean, strong muscles to power you every day of your life.

Finish Strong

How do you envision yourself down the road? Will you still be youthful, active, alert and full of health freedom? If you do, then you know you must prepare for the later stages of life.

Ask yourself these questions: "Who am I?" "Where am I now?" "Where do I desire to be in the future?" and, "Am I going to finish strong?"

Victor, Not a Victim

You may be facing serious health challenges right now, and feel you're on the verge of defeat. The mountains may appear too steep, the suffering too great to bear, and the odds far too long for victory, but I can say from personal experience as well as my experiences in helping others, it's probably way too early to give up.

Twice, I've been pronounced dead—no heartbeat, no respiratory function—I was shut down and torn apart. But thank God, my soul stayed alive and I'm still here writing these words today. By all accounts, given the gruesome injuries to my spinal cord, neck, back and legs—at best I should be half crippled and lucky to walk normally. The surgeons said I was done. I said I wasn't.

After some 20 years of an enlightening comeback against all odds, I've transformed myself from a doomed existence into one of the Top 25 fastest men over 55 years of age in America—*by putting the "Keys" into action.*

If you're still breathing, I'd say you don't need to walk in the valley of death just yet, and your chances are better than you think. When you think all is lost, know that's your opportunity to cross the threshold of doubt, and find yourself—and create a better you.

You don't need near death experiences or to test your will to survive to appreciate the life you have now. Live it, enrich it, and extend a hand to others. No matter what your situation, no matter how grave, you can mount a great comeback and move forward towards living your longest and doing good works every day until you reach your last.

To many, when a situation appears so bad, there may seem to be no logical way that this could be true—that you are simply doomed—but one's desire fueled by faith transforms the impossible to possible, and can knock logic aside, every time. With this mindset, you can become a victor, not a victim, and triumph over the challenges that pretend to bind you.

They Too Would Know

The scientific skeptics who shun the concepts of "faith" and "belief" because they both rely upon things unseen, smelled, measured or touched, have never experienced their miraculous manifestation, and the immense life transforming power, conveyed upon of those who do believe. The non-believers simply have no personal knowledge. If so, they too would know.

They claim that relying on "faith" is an intellectual dishonesty, living with the absence of reason and foolish hope clinging to empty promises based upon the untouchable and unseen. Who died and made them God? Well… that's their choice to "believe" that way, but it doesn't have to be yours. YOU are responsible and accountable for YOU. Do not consider, even for a second, violating your faith in yourself.

I have seen the triumph of belief over the so-called intelligence of science. You can overcome your serious health challenges AND become "younger" in the process.

Sometimes It Takes A Little Longer

One thing is certain, not all is certain in life. It is our job to handle what comes our way, and give meaning to it all. Be thankful for the unexpected, as it holds many blessings in disguise. As tough as it seems at the time, when we're presented with major challenges and total confusion, these are the times where we may gain our GREATEST insights and wisdom.

It is also when and where we discover our innermost strength and unrelenting belief in ourselves to overcome the supposedly insurmountable, the seemingly impossible, and the will to live our longest and best ever!

The state of faith allows no mention of impossibility. Faith moves mountains. Doubt creates them.

From what I've seen, the difficult stuff can usually be done pretty quick. It's the impossible things that can sometimes take a little longer.

The "Keys to Agelessness"

Essentially, effective Anti Aging can be amazingly low tech and certainly within your control. You can remarkably control your aging clock with marvelous efficiency with the "Ageless Keys" if you desire it, and believe it to be so.

Half hearted attention and application of the "keys" will render little results—but strong focus and application will send your results soaring!

And quite importantly, as you can already see, I am placing some serious personal responsibility on you to take charge of those things that you can control, that you can turn in your favor.

Please note: The following are merely a few abbreviated "Keys." For a more complete and expanded list, please visit: *www.AntiAgingNation.com*

Food: The Cellular Direct Connect

Obviously, we must eat to live. The question is, "how well do you desire to live?" Foods are your medicine; they are your tools, and they're also the construction building material that'll literally be you before you know it. Think of your body as a work in progress, and you are the architect of its design. You may look in the mirror and see a person growing older, but I'm here to tell ya', you're "just plain growing." Whether it's older though still youthful, well, that's up to you.

And, I'm not proposing a "perfect diet" for all because I don't believe there is one. However, I am stating that there's a NATURAL "cellular one-to-one direct connect" LIFE FORCE found within the rich nutrients in colorful, fresh, organic, enzyme active natural PLANT SOURCES from the land and sea, containing a variety of FRESH vegetables, fruits, healthy fats, lean flesh foods, nuts, seeds and herbs—as they naturally have specific cell site receptors in the body to go just where they're needed most.

Never forget; real, raw, fresh, "live" foods have a positive and high vibrational drive and help keep the body "alive." For most folks (not all, because of certain rare considerations), I'd suggest striving for around 75% raw fruits and vegetables in your diet. This may seem a rather high percentage to some but from what I've personally experienced, and witnessed around the world, the chances are the more "raw" you go, the farther you'll go too.

Marshmallows and Moon Pies

And of course, you must eliminate the junk foods, sodas, fast foods and chemically processed "Frankenfoods" that permeate the landscape. Processed packaged foods are created for shelf life—not human life. Other than being substances to stuff into your being, they do nothing but deaden you with their negative vibration. There's no way you can regenerate and rebuild your body's cells each day to stand strong and go the distance by filling it with negative nutrition trash. Marshmallows, Moon Pies and the like won't cut it.

Fuel your body right, and it'll drive you for one helluva ride through life. Fuel it wrong, and you'll be in the repair shop way too often from self inflicted damage. Keep treatin' it wrong, and you'll be in scrap heap hell.

Mindful Eating

Practice mindful eating—not mindless. Make sure you stop and think before you place something to eat or drink in your mouth. Ask yourself, "Will this food move me forward towards my goal of building my best health and longevity?" And, don't overeat.

Nutritional Supplements

There is no magic pill, potion, lotion or fountain of youth elixir that can keep you ageless just yet, though I and others are working on it. Until that time, nutritional supplements can be helpful boosters of health and longevity, and are a must in today's world. Modern farming (Agri Business) methods have depleted the vital nutrients from our soils and our foods. The nutrition is simply not fully there. Unfortunately, even with the best of food selection there are nutritional gaps, and it's virtually impossible to fully power your body without supplementing what you eat.

Active Exercise

A huge topic, but the main thing is movement. If you move youthfully, you'll remain young. And, always know that your muscles are the magic to remaining young and fit. You must also have a healthy self-image and a powerful and clear vision in your mind of your youthful physique in order for it to manifest. And by the way, ever seen an older person with muscles that didn't seem youthful?

When you employ the exercise "movements" regularly as suggested below, they'll do a great deal more than stimulate your muscles. There's a kind of "energetic flow" (vibration and frequency) that naturally occurs which allows for you to begin to firm up, make better food choices, develop positive habits and create the kind of mental mindset and focus that guides you to strength and success in many areas of your life. And, quite importantly, being fit and having a certain degree of physical power is necessary for you to live a full and comfortable life.

Keep You Strong

Life requires that we move against a bit of resistance. Always being soft about your movements won't keep you strong. In life we push, pull, reach, squat, lift, bend, extend and at times even jump or run – regardless of whether we play sports or we just handle the kids, groceries or a million other daily tasks. Be certain that your exercise employs all of these "movements" so that your body and heart will remain strong.

If you haven't exercised in a while—or ever—begin slowly and carefully as you incorporate moving against "resistance" into your life.

You don't need to be as "tough as an axe handle" about your exercise. Your purpose in exercise is not to be "bad to the bone" and punish your body, but to appropriately firm, strengthen and stimulate your body—as your primary intention is for it to last and go the distance.

Also, be sure to smoothly stretch several times throughout the day. If you sit on your job, get up at least every 15 to 30 minutes and smoothly walk and stretch for a minute or two.

As One

Be conscious of moving "rhythmically" (not necessarily slowly) and "feeling it deeply" no matter what "movement" you are doing. Train your mind to work with your body—not against it. Many people talk about the Mind–Body connection—being "as one"—but few truly master it.

Once you truly become "as one", you won't require "Spartan discipline" or any "super will power" whatsoever, and you will enter a realm of youth enhancing synergy where your metabolism becomes uniquely empowered toward overall anti aging cellular efficiency, promoting a very positive biochemical behavior within your body that provides for remarkable regeneration. It won't always be easy, though in time, your effort becomes "effortless effort."

Reduce Toxic Exposure

Toxic load from poor foods, toxic air we breathe (inside and outside), household chemicals, etc. Your body can never operate efficiently if it is besieged by toxins and harmful chemicals. NO smoking. Limit alcohol. A glass or two of red wine is fine, but don't cross the line.

Regular Eliminations

Your "personal plumbing"—as I call it — must be in good running order. Starting with good digestion, and ending with regular, healthy eliminations are a major key. Explore detoxification techniques.

Fresh Air

Breathe in some life. Deeply and often. Great for the body and soul. Explore deep breathing techniques for long life.

Moderate Sunshine

Letting the sun kiss you every so often just a little is a very sweet thing for superior health.

Hydrate Wisely

Don't let your radiator run low. Always stay on top of it. Use pure water and fresh healthy juices. Regulate your fluid intake according to your needs and activity. If you desire to remain young, be sure to hydrate wisely.

Proper Rest

One of your biggest allies in living your longest. Many vital processes to healthful living are occurring while you sleep. Getting sound, restful sleep (around 7 to 9 hours per night) also allows for a special overall cellular rejuvenation to take place that you just can't get anywhere else.

If your sleep is consistently thrown off, interrupted or generally poor, your body will suffer much more than the outward sign of just being tired. If you're not sleeping well, examine the physical and mental/emotional reasons why. Also, drugging yourself to sleep is a dead end. Think about it.

All wise men know that when you go to sleep at night you must do your best to release all the anger, bitterness, frustration and pain that may have built up during your day. If not, how can you experience the full promise and renewal of the new day to come?

Art of Slow

Seems everyone's got their own flow, their own pace in life, however, cultivating the art of "slow"—when there's no need to move fast—is a wise way to keep stress at bay, and appreciate all that is around you.

Healthy Blood Flow

You must have a pure, flowing river of healthy blood. You've got 70,000 miles of blood vessels, and they must flow freely. Poor circulation will eventually kill you. If your cells and tissues cannot properly receive oxygen and nutrients, as well as eliminate waste materials, you will rot and die inside. Not nice.

Stress – The Invisible Saboteur

Some stress can be beneficial, but stressful imbalance can be dangerously detrimental. I call stress the "invisible saboteur," the "assassin of health."

Stress can cause every disease in the medical dictionary—and shorten your lifespan. Indeed, there are biological beginnings to many diseases, but much of our physical condition, our physical state, is actually a transformation of our psychological sufferings... the emotional stresses, scars and pains we carry in our minds day by day, which manifest themselves in various forms of illness and degenerative disease.

Good Medicine

Laughter is an instant vacation. The power of forgiveness is immense. Strive to simplify your life. Pleasant words are like honey, sweet to the soul. Building healthy relationships does wonders for the mind and heart—literally. Give love, the most powerful force on earth.

It's been scientifically proven that caring for others, sharing your love, having a strong sense of purpose in your life and being happy will promote healthy cell regeneration and help you live a longer lifespan.

Look and Feel Reborn

Setting your goal to remain as youthful and vibrant for as long as you can, will provide you the opportunity to learn, to discover, and to know so much about yourself—so much more than just the pursuit of "living longer." All the many steps of employing the "Keys to Agelessness" will open your world to self awareness, to understanding your place in the universe, the impact you can have upon it, and in doing so, you will be amazed with all the good you can share with others, and also be amazed with finding the greatness within yourself.

When you exercise the fine art of merging the power of the mind with the practical, actual doing of the "keys", in many ways, you will look and feel reborn—and surely excel at living young.

Today is Your Day, Now is Your Time!

This is not an exhaustive list of all of the Keys to Agelessness as there's not enough space to pass along all of the health, fitness and longevity insights within the anti aging arsenal that I share when mentoring my clients. But, no matter—Just Get Started.

Today is your day, now is your time! This is your call to action. You don't need to be perfect, just passionate, and just get it going. Your life can live strong from this moment on, and living long can become a positive, self-fulfilling prophecy.

From Here To Eternity

It's time to take a stand for your health, longevity and life—as well as the lives of your loved ones. Join me on this journey of discovery, learning and growing younger—so you can BE ALIVE while you are living. For more information and a more complete list of "Keys", you can go to: *www. AntiAgingNation.com* or *www.SteveJennings.com.*

You may not live forever, but shooting for it can help you live your longest, strongest, and most fulfilling life—one in which you author your own story of happiness and health filled longevity.

Whatever it is in this book that speaks to YOU apply it. And SHARE it with others, so that they too may live stronger, longer and more fulfilling lives.

And, one final key: Live your life so that the good legacy you leave will last as long as time endures, and live on from here to eternity.

Steve Jennings is one of the nation's leading authorities on health, longevity, business productivity and peak human performance. A highly regarded business consultant to the Natural Products industry, Steve has directed projects with many of America's top health and nutrition companies. And, as one of today's most prominent figures in the field of Anti-Aging, he is also a highly recognized advocate for Baby Boomers and those over 40 as it relates to important political, social, governmental and economic perspectives.

Steve is also a Nationally ranked track and field sprinter—one of the Top 25 fastest men in America over the age of 55. Visit *www.AntiAgingNation.com* or *www.SteveJennings.com*

Published by FastPencil
http://www.fastpencil.com